The PseudoPod Tapes Vol 2

Alasdair Stuart

www.foxspirit.co.uk

Cover Art by Jonathan M. Chaffin
HorrorInClay.com
Twitter@CthulhuMug

conversion by handebooks.co.uk

ISBN: 978-1-910462-08-9

A Fox Spirit Original
Fox Spirit Books
www.foxspirit.co.uk
adele@foxspirit.co.uk

Contents

JANUARY

SOUNDTRACKS OF FICTIONAL LONDON

Capital Ghosts

*(This essay originally appeared on PseudoPod episode 315, "**Bad Company**" by Walter de la Mare, narrated by Paul Jenkins on March 18th 2013. Due to an accident of scheduling, this episode actually ran in March, but is included here because this was its originally-intended position.)*

London has a gravitational pull. As someone not so much Northern as one part Northern, one part Celto-Viking I push against that good and hard, but it's true. The first time I was in London was a family holiday, delayed and removed from our usual venue of York by a family bereavement. It was a cultural bank raid; in, see some things, out, in a long weekend.

I think, with the benefit of hindsight, it changed my life. I mean, look at some of the things I got to do.

I had a whole hotel room to myself.

I stayed up past 9.

PM.

And there were *still* TV programs on.

I watched Jonathan Ross.

He had Norman Lovett from Red Dwarf on.

They swore.

IT WAS AMAZING.

The thing that amazed me more than anything else, aside from Ross' suits of course, was the pace. I was and still am an island boy, used to a place that's ninety percent fields and where ten cars on a mile of road was congestion. The road outside our hotel room had three lanes of traffic going in both directions, 24 hours a day. I sat at my window and watched it, an asphalt artery, pumping citizens around one of those places I'd only seen in the films I wasn't really allowed to watch.

I walked fast. I ate fast. I talked fast. I held the firehose of information that was the city against my face and opened my mouth as wide as I possibly could. London grabbed me, pulled me in and spat me back out, a gravitational sling shot of culture that threw me into my teens at near light speed.

Each time I went back it was the same. Visits to family or friends, visits to the theatre, a weekend spent hanging out in

Borough Market surrounded by a cornucopia of fresh food and creativity. Every time I've been to London it's woken me up. I've always seen something else, always found myself more aware not only of my surroundings, but their context. Sometimes it's been the instinctive pushback of an island boy in the big city. Sometimes it's been realizing that every street I'm walking along has seen history made on it. Sometimes, it's been buying cake for protestors outside St Paul's.

And sometimes, it's the ghosts of the city that stay with me.

Like London itself, they're almost ludicrously diverse. Rulers, politicians, soldiers, beggars and everything in-between. Each city street is crammed full of people and, next to them, the people you can never see but are always there. Iain Sinclair talks, at often incomprehensible length, about the idea of cities as crystallized time and London is a perfect example of that. On this side of the street, a bomb site, on that, the location of the first female-run Boxing federation in the world. Come for the history, stay for the fight card-styled menus. Leave because of the prices.

But if the ghosts of London are so numerous, then the ghosts of London need police too. This is where things get really interesting, as history and fiction mix with each other. London is an idea of a city, a postmodern hive of memory and knowledge and its policemen are as numerous as they are oddly familiar.

Dixon of Dock Green patrols the same streets as Dempsey and Makepeace, Bodie and Doyle and the Sun Hill police station. The same streets that, in the 1980s, saw Gene Hunt and his team yell at criminals even as Hunt struggled to not look in the eyes what he truly was.

Hunt's not alone either. Ben Aaronovitch's *Rivers of London* series is based around a pair of police officers who investigate the more unusual and occult crimes of the capital city, whilst Paul Cornell's *London Falling* takes a subtly different approach, as a team of London coppers discover the truth about their city. Finally, *Absalom* by Tiernan Trevellion and Gordon Rennie is a series about Harry Absalom, the police officer whose team helps enforce London's treaty with Hell and what happens when that treaty starts to break down. Down these mean streets and all that.

What fascinates me about these series is the common ground they share with other stories set in the city. The bizarre secret societies of *Kraken* by China Mieville could fit in perfectly happily here, and who's to say one of these officers didn't serve with Gene Hunt? Either as a live officer or as the grumpy, Mancunian Charon he would become?

This isn't my usual postmodern sugar rush either. Absalom explicitly says he worked with Charlie Barlow from *Z-Cars* and Jack Regan from *The Sweeney*. That ties the comic to those two shows, the sequel *Softly, Softly* and the several shows that followed it. Crucially it also brings them forward in history and opens up the possibility of these characters working with Rockcliffe of *Rockcliffe's Babies*, or even Martin Schenk, the veteran DSU from *Luther*.

Here's where it gets really interesting though, at least for me. There are two Jack Regans, one from the 1970s show and one from the recent movie. There are ways to explain this of course. Superheroes are ideas, and, like V said, ideas are bulletproof. But the men and women under the costumes are not. There will always be *A* Jack Regan. But it won't always be the same one.

He's not the only one either. There are multiple Sherlock Holmes in multiple time periods and zones, not to mention the characters like Monk and Luther who are clearly inspired by, or at the very least owe a debt, to him. All of them ghosts of the mind, policing ghosts of the urban.

London is a blank slate that millions of people have written their name on, stories built on stories like buildings built on buildings and the end result is that sometimes things, and people, fall through the cracks. When they do, that's when these officers go to work, standing between us and harm, whether physical or metaphorical.

London has a gravitational pull. It's a city where as many stories walk the streets as people. I find it reassuring those stories are defended too.

I will drag your clan to glory whether you like it or NOT.-
Urdnot Wrex, Mass Effect 3

Striking The Chords

*(This essay originally appeared on PseudoPod episode 316, "**The Persistence of Memory**" by William Meikle, narrated by Christiana Ellis on January 11th 2013)*

I saw Elbow in concert a few weeks ago. They've got this incredible combination of orchestration and lean rock composition that's all tied together with Guy Garvey's voice. Garvey has one of the most extraordinary voices on the planet, his range is vast and there's something completely honest about the emotion behind everything he sings. He's also very, very funny live, an effortlessly charming Northern frontman with a deadpan wit and the sort of comic timing I dream of having.

Also?

He's a big gentleman who's confident, funny and looks good in a suit.

Let's just say I took notes.

Elbow have been the on and off soundtrack of the last few years of my life. I can remember the first place I saw the video for 'Leaders of the Free World' and I can definitely remember sitting in a McDonalds listening to 'Grounds for Divorce' on a very, very bad day. It's like they say in *The Bones of You*:

When out of a doorway the tentacles stretch of a song that I know
and the world moves in slow-mo.
Straight to my head like the first cigarette of the day.

I spent November doing NanoJourno, my version of NaNoWriMo and I did very well. I ended up writing 135, 703 words of journalism that month and every day when I hit my goal, I'd listen to *Ray Charles* by Chiddy Bang. Because it's the song the Alamo Drafthouse plays over its 'Here's what's coming' trailer which I saw for the first time in Texas with Marguerite and one of my closest friends, Whit, during the Summer I lived in the US. It's a glorious, bouncy, swaggery track and it always takes me back to that moment, in that building, in that company.

Music makes you honest, whether you need it to or not. And sometimes that's terrifying. There was one track Elbow played, *Everyone's Here*, which almost reduced me to a snotty, bubbling wreck in a room full of 5000 other people. It's a wonderful, sweeping, orchestral piece of music about the pure, grounded joy of being able to lean on your friends and family when you're broken down. There's one line in particular;

You're not the man who fell to Earth, you're the man of La Mancha

That's actually making me teary now. My ability to feel faith in myself, let alone in others is a little damaged sometimes. So between that line and the repeated chorus of 'Everyone's Here', and the fact that, for me, and for so many of us, not everyone is, I'm basically a wreck by the end of the song.

But that's a good thing.

Music renders us down. It makes us look at ourselves. It's our better angels, wings flapping in perfect pitch, telling us what we need to see and sometimes making us look. It's wonderful and terrible and completely, utterly essential to us. That makes it something that can tear us apart or something that can make us invincible. It's why fighters have entrance themes, why movie trailers hit us where we live. We all get a soundtrack. We all get a story. Make yours a great one.

The Song Remains The Same, And Is Often Annoying

*(This essay originally appeared on PseudoPod episode 317, "**Enzymes**" by Greg Stolze, narrated by Kyle Akers on January 18th 2013)*

I've been thinking a lot about one particular issue of *Sandman* recently. It's the one that introduces Hob Gadling, the man who lives forever because he's decided to and because he happens to have this conversation in earshot of Death and Dream. It's a great story, elegantly constructed and using the recurrent motif of Dream meeting him every hundred years to show how things have changed for Hob, his highs and dismal lows and how despite all of them he refuses to break, refuses to give in. Because he's human and that's what we do.

The thing I like about it isn't Hob himself, but rather the structure, the idea that the more things change the more they stay basically the same. It's actually fed back into my interest in Psychogeography. Psychogeography is the topography of fiction, the way that certain types of stories naturally exist on the same cloth. So, to return to everyone's favourite cockney mean streets, Ben Aaronovtich's *Rivers of London*, Paul Cornell's *London Falling* and Gordon Rennie and Tiernan Trevellion's excellent *Absalom* series don't just co-exist, they do so in the same fictional landscape as classic British cop shows like *Z Cars* and *The Sweeney*. Which in turn co exists happily with its 2012 big screen remake, just as, a couple of police stations over John Luther waits for a call from John Munch at SVU in New York whilst nearby John's sidekick, Justin, reads about the fate of a police officer in Liverpool who looked almost exactly like him and, a few more stations over, another officer with a startling resemblance to Justin leads an off-the-books team in a series of increasingly daring sting operations.

All the same place, none of the same stories. And don't even get me started on how there can be two men, both called

Sherlock Holmes, active on different sides of the Atlantic at the same time…

It happens in life too. I always remember spending a couple of years being associated with the Science Fiction and Fantasy Society at York University. I didn't go there but my then girlfriend did and a lot of my closest friends were part of that particular circle. It was great and what was even greater, in many ways, was going back a few years later.

Because the same people were there, just a few years younger. Seriously it was like Geek Trek: The Next Generation. There was the smart one, there was the carefully misanthropic one, over there was the one trying to work out if they were gay, the one who knew they were gay and were trying to figure out if anyone minded and round again. The same music played by different instruments.

The thing about music is that sometimes certain instruments get lost in the overall sound. I date a timpanfuhrer (*Cast of Wonders*, Episode 24: *Kulturkampf* by Anatoly Belilovsky, will explain) and I know all too well how music is built, rather than played, each note building on the ones before it until you find yourself wrapped in a structure of brass and strings, woodwind and chord. We hear the symphony but take a single instrument out and all we hear is the gap.

That's where some truly great horror lives, including the story that this piece was originally attached to. There's immense, nasty fun to be had focusing on the instruments we don't normally hear. You get an idea of how the music is structured, how important those instruments are. The Rosencrantz and Guildensterns of creativity, the things we always ignore until they're gone. There's heroism in a bass line and reassurance in an old melody played with new hands. And there's always music. Always.

Maps

*(This essay originally appeared on PseudoPod episode 318, "**Venice Burning**" by A. C. Wise, narrated by Ben Phillips on January 25th 2013)*

I finally MP3'ed all my CDs. This was both an impressive feat and an impressive feat of work avoidance, but in my defence, I'll point to the 135,703 words I wrote last month and how many of them weren't rude. The CD process took a while but about halfway through it became fascinating because it became archaeology. I found albums I hadn't touched, let alone played, for years and in converting them over, I found myself able to re-open conversations with them. Like the cluster of Trip Hop and dance that I picked up in the late 1990s, or my brief, profound love affair with all sorts of nu metal. It's similar to a couple of years ago when I found an old mp3 player I hadn't used for a while and listened back to the playlist. It was like having a conversation with myself from five years in the past and being pleasantly surprised by how much I'd changed. Music opens doors on old memories and they're often not the doors you'd expect them to be.

Doorways to other memories, and other places. Doorways which can close behind us if we let them and trap us in the never ending, cycling emotions of our worst memories, our lowest days. I know far too many people trapped behind those doors. Their numbers don't need to be added to. Like I said, there's always music. And, take it from someone who on the bad days still has trouble believing this, you can always change it.

'...months later as I sat in a juvenile detention home rereading those poems that had opened up the artist in me I was blindsided by the raging fist of my incarcerator who informed me that Walt Whitman's homoerotic unnatural pornographic sentiments were unacceptable and would not be allowed in an institution dedicated to reforming the ill-formed.

Chris Stephens, Northern Exposure

FEBRUARY

HOUSEKEEPING IN PLACE

The Calls Have Always Been Coming From Inside Your Brain

*(This essay originally appeared on PseudoPod episode 319, "**Cell Call**" by Marc Laidlaw, narrated by George Cleveland on February 1st 2013)*

There's a unique flavour of horror that I never really see enough of, I suspect because, appropriately, it's shadowy territory. The basic tone is located a couple of levels above 'The calls are coming from inside the house!' and about nine below 'Sookie! You're half Fae and your brother's a werepanther! And why is there a huge pile of my clothes burning on the lawn?' and the best way to describe it is the Quiet Horrific. It's that slick, oily moment where you realize reality has taken a left turn and you've *Yosemite Sam*'ed right off the edge of the film strip and you're still running.

For.

Now.

True horror, as William Friedkin once said, is seeing something approach. Perhaps here, true horror is seeing something that should be yours but isn't. A predator's camouflage that looks great but is a little too bright, smiles a little too widely, shows too many teeth. It's the moment before the trap shuts but the moment you see the bars. The punch is chambered but not thrown. The prey is caught but doesn't know it.

Yet.

That idea of holding back from the conclusion, of showing something jump, but not land, is one of the bravest things any writer will ever do. Make no mistake, we all want everything on the page, want everything clear and concise and laid out and this stuff's in our head so it damn well better be in yours too. But sometimes you need to leave gaps, sometimes you need to trust your audience. Sometimes you don't so much need to kill your darlings as you do have them exeunt stage left, pursued by a bear. If you can do that, and make it work, then you're going to chill an audience in the best way possible. Don't believe me? I'm alone in the house on a pitch-black Nottingham afternoon and just WRITING about this stuff has given me goosebumps.

I love it. This story is a perfect example of it. More please.

You've Got This

*(This essay originally appeared on PseudoPod episode 320, "**The Man with the Broken Soul**" by Matt Wall, narrated by Elie Hirschman on February 8th 2013)*

I'm having a good day today. I've done two loads of laundry, I've tidied and cleaned, I've written up a couple of endcaps, done some research, made some cheese and mustard bread. Worked out how big cheese and mustard bread gets when you leave it to prove and discovered that I can do pretty rock-solid chicken Dim Sum too.

Of course, there's still stuff to do. There's this little wipe-clean noticeboard to the left of my screen that currently has the half of the blog tour to promote the book I still need to do written on it. Underneath that is the word ENDCAPS! With a couple of lines under it. Chill tiny board, I'm getting there.

Then there's three book reviews to finish, four RPG reviews to start, a short story to close out (Yes I know I'm *Mr Doesn't Do Fiction* anymore. Shut up, don't make eye contact with it) and, and, and, and, and...

I could - and have been, for years in the past - been so consumed with doing a little bit of one thing that I never actually get anything done. That old story about the frog jumping half each previous jump and never quite getting to the pond springs to mind.

It's very easy to want to do everything. And it's even easier to want to do everything at once because when you push yourself past your limits, extraordinary things happen. I've pulled all-nighters before now, and I've done at least some of my share of holding onto an equally exhausted opponent after ten minutes of Judo Randori, waiting for the session to end. You grow by pushing, you grow by working. You grow, to some extent through conflict and drama. And not through tea, cakes and civilised conversation. Well, at least not as fast as you should do.

You grow by pushing, not by standing still or worse,

moving backwards. The word growth is wrapped around the concept of movement like a vine. You can't have one without the other and you can't learn, you can't finish anything, if your attention is divided. It's an act of courage comparable to taking that first step on pretty much anything. See it through, don't get distracted and keep going. You've got this. And so have I.

All Systems Banquo

*(This essay originally appeared on PseudoPod episode 321, "**I Am the Box, the Box is Me**" by Kyle S. Johnson, narrated by Pete Milan on February 15th 2013)*

We encode ourselves on the places we live. We write our histories across them with crayon and blood, tears and ink and before we know it we've created a masterpiece. I worked in that building. I saw someone steal from the bookshop that used to be in that building. That building used to have squatters who were there so long they were able to print a newsletter with weekly updates on their inevitably futile war with the council. History in memories. The geography of a life.

But sometimes you paint yourself into a corner. Sometimes you find yourself surrounded by your own work with no idea how to add something new to it without damaging everything else. Sometimes something so unutterably traumatic happens that the event stains a place, leaves part of you behind. A lot of people have places they don't want to go, things they don't want to be reminded of. I'm one of them. I'm willing to bet you are too.

We leave a piece of ourselves there and when we do that we lessen ourselves. Do that often enough, there's nothing left but the empty, fading echo of something you used to be. A stone tape ghost, listening to the sounds around it and wondering why it can't remember where it is, how it got there, or who it was. Endlessly being. Endlessly static. Not Hell, but close enough. Don't paint yourself into a corner, or if you do, make sure it's a really, really good corner.

THE MEN IN BLACK

*(This essay originally appeared on PseudoPod episode 322, "**Cry Room**" by Ted Kosmatka, narrated by Peter Piazza on February 22nd 2013. It was a joint promotion with Nightmare Magazine.)*

In the UK there is a very long-running series of radio plays that have had several titles. *Appointment with Fear, Fear on Four* and most recently, if I remember correctly, just *The Man in Black*. That gentleman has been played by several actors over the years, all portraying him as a supernatural, laconic presence who wanders up from the basement of Broadcasting House once a week to tell you something terrible. The ones I know best, from the '80s saw the Man in Black played by Valentine Dyall. He was a laconic, assured, funny host who would set up the events of the story for you and then come back at the end with a witty, stinging rejoinder.

The stories were fantastic, beautifully set up little one-off pieces of horror and there was one in particular about a woman, on holiday alone, deciding to climb a tower on one side of a small Spanish valley. If I remember correctly much was made of how she was frightened of risks and was goaded into climbing the tower at night, despite the local legends that the devil would trap you forever if you didn't count the right number of steps.

There were around 500 steps.

The episode finished with, terrified by something I can't remember on top of the tower, her running for it. The last thing you heard before the Man in Black made his return was her tearfully whispering '700, 701, 702…' as the steps went down and down forever…

Horror is always sitting behind you, horror is always the room that shouldn't be there, the steps that there shouldn't be room for. Horror is patient and forever and implacable. A Man in Black always observing the nightmares but never once stepping in to help. He's still around by the way, the role passing to Mark Gatiss, not only a writer but a horror historian in his own right. I wonder if he counts the stairs in strange towers. I know I have.

So here's to the Men in Black. To Valentine Dyall and Mark Gatiss. To Alex Cox, whose *Moviedrome* series taught me everything that *Fear on Four* didn't. To fellow Manx movie analyst Mark Kermode from whom I once won six Wim Wenders movies in a field in Yorkshire. To Nige and Steph of *Vids*, the foul-mouthed, brilliantly worded video review show that taught me the best afterlife is filled with biscuits and began my education in Giallo horror. To them and every other host and master of ceremonies. Of the action but not in the action. On the stage but not in the play. In the spotlight but not in control of it. They have the best stories.

..away from the blood in their eyes and the blood in their hearts, for the blood turning dry on his hands.
The Preacher by Jamie N Commons

March

All or Nothing

Why I Fight

*(This essay originally appeared on PseudoPod episode 323, "**The Trinket**" by P. G. Bell, narrated by John Trevillian on March 1st 2013)*

I last practiced any form of martial art in a hall in California. We attended a Krav Maga session run by an Air Force officer as endlessly cheerful as he was pathologically incapable of not trying to kill us with physical exercise. It was an interesting experience, because Krav Maga, as he viewed it, isn't a martial art. There are no Kata, no set forms, certainly basically no rules of competition. Instead, Krav Maga is focused on one thing, getting you away from your attacker as fast as possible, with the possibility of doing your attacker crippling damage on the way out a real plus.

In the space of an hour, we learnt three or four different ways to chain blows together, a couple of decent trips and throws that tied nicely into my Judo and Marguerite's Aikido training and did enough cardio to remind me that I hadn't gone running in entirely too long. It was huge fun, and hugely difficult, and it was, for an hour focused entirely on violence, entirely positive.

I'm not kidding, some of the most polite people I've ever met have been in dojos. Martial artists start out as an uneasy combination of terror and ego, absolutely convinced they're the baddest son of a bitch in the room and completely terrified of having to prove it. Some of them of course are fully capable of proving it, as I found out during a Judo drill where a French colleague of mine basically spent ten minutes fighting and pinning the entire opposite team, in order, more than once. It actually got to the point where one of the black belts jokingly asked if the rest of us just wanted to bow off and wait for Albert to finish. Albert, I think, laughed. In fairness he was a little busy choking his fourth consecutive opponent into submission that minute and I was a little busy riding the wave of '…I'M ALIVE!!!!' euphoria that always came from stepping off the mat after sparring.

But in my limited experience, guys like that are the exception to the rule. The vast majority of the people who've taught me have been polite, friendly, endlessly positive and patient. Now, it being me that of course turns into 'They're coddling the fat guy' in my mind. I'm working on that, especially as it's looking like our lives are finally settling down enough to make regular training a real possibility. I feel no need to go back to Muay Thai, and there's no Judo club I can find in the area, but there is, a mile and a half away, a Brazilian Jujitsu club. They're a part of a worldwide organization, they're local, their rates are cheap and they seem welcoming.

Which means, two weeks or so out, before we can go along, I find myself asking…myself, the same question that the story does.

What do you fight for?

A couple of years ago I had a plan. I was going to grade a couple of times in Judo, get my Thai boxing decent and take just one cage fight. Just to see if I could. That made perfect sense at the time, because there were things going on in my life which meant it was, perennially, out of control. And, I now realize, I was both supremely angry and very interested in actually getting some form of physical catharsis. With that in mind the idea of the simple, disciplined math of me and another guy in an octagon was pretty attractive.

Then, two days out from my first Judo tournament, a bad throw injured my knee for eight months. I watched my training partner, the only other person in my weight class, win simply by stepping onto the mat. Had I been able to put my gi on, the fight would have been very simple; Steve would have politely, and firmly, picked me up, put me on my ass and pinned me. And I've got a silver medal, shitty knee and all.

But I could barely walk, let alone fight. So I sat on the side lines and got wounded all over again simply by being there. You know that slightly hysterical laugh you do when something has stabbed you in the gut and twisted a bit and the other option is screaming? Yeah? Did that.

A few months later, my life changed completely. The reasons for the anger, the reasons for the self-loathing and my obligation to remain in the town I'd lived in for 18 years all went away. I bowed off the mat, in more ways than one.

I may not go back.

There are days when that really bothers me. Sometimes quite a lot of them in quick succession. One of the things no one tells you when you walk around on alternating sides of 300 pounds and at 6'2 is that your physical activity choices are somewhat limited. Martial arts, along with yoga and running (But that's a story for another time) are the only things I've really connected with. The thought of never going back is, honestly, depressing some days.

But if I don't…that's okay. I think. Because that's not why I fight.

I fight to define myself, every day, against a lifetime of expectations and slights, perceived and real. I fight to get my voice heard over my own crippling self-doubts and occasional self-loathing. I fight to keep going when professional frustration ties me so tightly in knots that I sit and seethe, or cry, or just get so numbed to any professional development that I don't let myself feel the joy because everything takes so damn long because EVERYONE ELSE ISN'T ME.

I fight to be recognised for the work I do, and I burn when I'm not. I fight to be respected and expect not to be, but that, I see, is based on past experience rather than current truth. I fight to move aside from the countless times I've been let down, across the board, in the past, and focus on all the times things have come through. I fight to have faith, in myself, in my work, in other people.

I fight because if you don't fight the only thing you're doing is standing still. And sooner or later, you'll have to fight to do that too.

I fight because I write. I write because that's how I fight. And I don't need a mat, a cage or a ring for that. I just need this.

'The cage is your home. You set the pace. You set the rhythm. Feel the Beethoven. Be smarter than him, more patient. Wait for him to make a mistake. And when he does, that's your moment. '
Warrior, Frank Campana

The Henchman Blues

*(This essay originally appeared on PseudoPod episode 324, "**Wings**" by Nathaniel Lee, narrated by John Bell on March 8th 2013)*

There's a line in an old Ed Mcbain novel I love. Mcbain, who also wrote under his actual name, Evan Hunter, was terrifyingly prolific and when he was on point, he was phenomenal. You can actually trace the evolution of the police procedural thriller through his work, starting with the gloriously tatty green Penguin paperbacks of his early work to the slickly produced, die cut hardbacks of his final years. His stuff varies wildly from massively stereotypical to grounded, pragmatic and humane. If you liked *Homicide: Life on the Street*, or *The Wire* then you'll find things to enjoy in Mcbain's books. Of course there's also a fair amount of tat, but rough with the smooth.

There's an early one of his books where, three quarters of the way through, the criminal is apprehended. Not by the two main characters but by a uniform cop who pulls him over for a minor violation. The case is done, wound up, finished and the final quarter of the book is the aftermath. It's particularly great because the detectives, who, by definition, buy into the narrative of their job (Good guy vs bad guy, good guy wins) spend a lot of time working out the psychological math of what's just happened. It all boils down, if I remember correctly, to a single line:

'Everyone thinks they're the hero of their story.'

Dorothy is the heroine of her story because of what she perceives. The Wicked Witch is the heroine of her story because of what she goes through. The wizard is the hero because of what's he's done and what's done to him. There are no henchmen, there are no secondary characters, there is just a never-ending chorus of heroes and heroines, protagonists and leads, screaming at the author, and the reader, to be heard. That old saw about how an author has to struggle with their muse? That's crap.

But the image of the author trying to pick the right voices

out of the cacophony of people in their head trying to be heard? That has some appeal.

The Woods, Today

*(This essay originally appeared on PseudoPod episode 325. Featuring "**Entrance and Exit**" by Algernon Blackwood, narrated by David Rees-Thomas, and "The Terror of the Twins" by Algernon Blackwood, narrated by Simon Meddings on March 15th 2013)*

The stiff upper lip, the tendency the British have to not show emotion, is unfortunately very real. It's as though, at times, the country is suspended in a fragile web of decorum that allows us all to function and make small talk and only recoil in horror from our lives a little bit and behind closed doors. If the web remains intact, then everyone remains numb, and safe. If the web breaks, suddenly the country may have to feel something and that way madness lies!

Marguerite has a favourite cartoon. It's just one panel and its two people, one sitting down at a breakfast table, the other standing. The person standing is saying:

Would you like some tea?

The person sitting is saying

No

And the caption is ANARCHY IN THE UK.

It's funny because it's true.

But interesting things happen when that web breaks, and it breaks more often than you might think. I've spent my life surrounded by people who've had the courage to look the paranormal, or at the very least the unexplained, in the eye. I've had friends who've experimented with Ouija boards, friends who've lost time.I had four friends at University who had exactly the same experience in four separate places, each time involving a horrific and very specific dream of their own deaths. The rationalist part of me wants to explain that as collective hysteria. The part of me that understands why they apologise when they cross to the south side of the city doesn't want to think too hard about it.

There's still primal woodland in this country. Still places you can go where there's no one else, where you can feel nature looking back at you through a dozen smaller sets of eyes. There are still places which feel calm, still, unwelcoming. The UK is a campfire around which its inhabitants cluster, making sure to only look at the fire and the people around it and to laugh a little too loudly to cover the sound of what's moving out there in the darkness. That's the real stiff upper lip, the refusal to look horror in the fact not out of cowardice but because once you do it's all you can ever see. There's courage there, as well as terror, madness and beauty.

Because when you do turn away from the fire, it's even odds as to whether you'll be destroyed or remade. That way addiction lies, and madness. But so does knowledge and if there's one thing this country, of which I am at least nominally a citizen (Manx boys represent, yo) loves more than emotional shutdown, its knowledge. So if you want to learn, you take walks through old woods, or stay up past midnight. You work out what lies behind Blackwood's beautiful, minimalist, chilling phrasing and you do your best not to think too hard about it. You accept that you're probably never quite alone and never will be.

There's a moment in Neil Gaiman's *Books of Magic* mini-series where Tim Hunter, the boy destined to be the greatest magic user of his age, is told he has a choice; let magic into his life and danger with it or live in a safe, dull world. He's told this, at least in part, by John Constantine, a man who either owes John Silence a drink or twenty quid, and Tim spends much of the book mulling the choice over. When he makes it, the moment is transformative, revelatory and just a little dark, much like the woods and library of Blackwood's stories. Dangerous, but beautiful.

Algernon Blackwood. John Silence. John Constantine. Tim Hunter. Harry Potter.

Magic runs through the veins of this country. And the stiff upper lip? We've developed that to stop from grinning at how happy that makes us.

'There's no such thing as silence'
This seems to be a reference to John Cage's '4'33', a silent composition that's been famously covered by countless musicians.

Nothing is True. Everything is Permitted.

*(This essay originally appeared on PseudoPod episode 326, "**Bunraku**" by David X. Wiggin narrated by John Chu on March 22nd 2013)*

We believe what we want to believe and see what we want to see and that changes on a daily basis. I went through a phase, a couple of weeks ago, where I didn't want to look at myself in mirrors because I was getting paranoid about my weight. Again. A couple of weeks prior to that there were a couple of songs I had to play every day to ensure the narrative of my life was correctly soundtracked. Those same songs have, briefly, landed on the IF YOU PLAY THIS IT WILL BE LIKE THE RING SOUNDTRACKED BY BRUCE SPRINGSTEEN LIST too.

Reality is consensual, the only consensus you need is your own and that consensus is often not readily available and never ever stable. Don't believe me? Woken up every single morning of your life feeling a million dollars? No? Didn't think so.

Now if I go too far down this path then we end up at the 'All you have to do is think positive!' school of thought. Spending your life being Mary Poppins is about as useful as spending your life being Marilyn Manson, it's just the clothes are lighter and there are more cup-cakes. Both extremes are also fundamentally self-delusional. Not everything is perfect and lovely and adorable and not everything is shit and grim and relentless and if I can say that in ENGLAND? In MARCH? Then it has to be true.

That's what cuts us off from each other, those extremes, those needs to be one thing or the other. The simple truth, and like all simple truths it's the hardest thing in the world to under-stand, is that we're whatever we choose to be, whatever we want, or need, to be. Sometimes we need to hide from the world, just like the lead does here, to wrap ourselves around our partner and make them our universe. Sometimes all we need, all we can hope for, is the touch of someone's skin against ours, a hand grasping our own. Sometimes all we want to do is stay there, because it doesn't matter if the person's real, it matters that they're real to you. As one half of a formerly long distance, now short distance, relationship, I can absolutely relate to that.

But you can't step out from society forever. You can take breaks though, and in the case of some parts of society they can be extended ones. I'm around a year, with one, awful exception, out from my last visit to Mass and with the Catholic Church's hierarchy singing ever louder to cover the sound of files being shredded and bags being packed I'm not going back anytime soon. The church's personal reality is clouded by decades of hypocrisy and ignorance, and mine? My skies are a lot clearer these days.

That's where true horror lies for me. Not in the love of an idea or a performance because I'm a writer for God's sake how can I dare have an issue with that? No, the real horror lies in the wilful and deliberate refusal of many to see the world outside the idea, outside the performance. Their sun and moon, their universe revolves around the performance and the ephemeral gossamer web it has them all trapped in. That's not a refuge, that's a voluntary coma and it can only end in death, be it spiritual or real.

Wake up. Change your state. Do something new. The world's a strange place. Keep it that way.

You're So Much Stronger Than You Think You Are

*(This essay originally appeared on PseudoPod episode 327, "**What It's Come To**" by Wolf Hartman, narrated by Zhames Tremarco on March 29th 2013)*

The end of the world is something we're all fascinated by on some level, for the same reason some people pick fights, some people climb mountains and some people jump out of perfectly good aeroplanes. The same instinct that drives us to strive to seek to find and not to yield drives us to push, to invade, to subjugate and control. After all, knowledge is power.

But sometimes ignorance isn't bliss.

Sometimes ignorance is seeing fires over the horizon, hearing laughter. Sometimes ignorance is every lie we tell ourselves; that we'll be brave and strong and kind, beaten out of us with iron bars. Human bodies are soft, and very easy to break if you know where. I always remember being told what to do when I was being bullied at school. All six foot one and 200 plus pounds of me;

Hit them.

Break their nose. It'll hurt. It'll bleed. They'll stay away from you.

They probably would have too. But that word, that 'probably' is a long dark alleyway where people go to lick their wounds and come back with scars and the desire to make more. The choice I was faced with, aged 11, wasn't whether the bullying would stop but what theatre the bullying would take place in; psychological or physical.

Physical wasn't an arena I was comfortable with. And, honestly, I'm still not. Off the mat I've never been in a fight. Like I said, 6'1 200 plus pounds. It's the perk.

So I endured it and it was awful for far longer than simply getting beaten up would have been. Kids are evil, when they want to be and being the size I was meant I was the target for four or five them. Men who, due to the tiny community I grew up in, I still know. Men who I still won't spend time around because of what they did to me and what I let them do.

But, and it stuns me to even be writing this, there was an upside to what they did. While I was waiting them out, while I was internalizing my rage I built the rich internal fantasy life that led to me becoming a writer, a journalist and a podcaster. I learnt endurance instead of bravery, patience instead of aggression and when things in my life got bad, and they did, all that happened was I internalised more and more and more. Remember the dream architecture Dom and Mal build in Inception? My brain looked a lot like that for a long, long time.

The human body is very easy to break. The human spirit can take damage like you wouldn't believe. All the lies you tell yourself are cut and burnt and ripped away until the only thing that's left is what's in front of you and how you react to it. And believe me, three times out of six? That reaction will not make you proud to look in the mirror. Survival isn't honour. Survival is necessity.

But it's just damage. It's just hurt. There's a Frank Miller quote I love, and I know those are in short supply these days, but this is a doozy. It goes:

"The noir hero is a knight in blood-caked armour. He's dirty and he does his best to deny the fact that he's a hero the whole time."

These days I'd argue you can lose the noir from that. There's another quote, I've heard attributed to Mohammed Ali.

Everyone has a plan till they get punched in the face.

We all get punched in the face. We all get beaten and stepped on and worked over by life and the only reason it stops is the only reason it starts; BECAUSE. Because everyone gets it at random times and to complete the quote trifecta for the week, as Christopher Walken as Gabriel once put it the only thing you can ever rely on is never knowing why.

Which renders your life down to two choices. Surrender, or stand.

There is no bravery in losing your shit, in surrendering to Chaos, to anarchy, to living in the land of do as you please. There is so much courage, so much bravery in picking your line and not being pushed past it. You will not be thanked. You'll probably get beat some more. But that doesn't matter. What matters is you stand. What matters is you endure until you can't or until it stops. I promise you, I swear on my own experience and on the experience of people I know that almost every single time it will stop before you run out of courage. And if you don't have courage. You have endurance. And that brings us to our last quote this week, from Grant Morrison's All Star Superman. A young woman is getting ready to jump off a building and, suddenly, Superman is standing behind her. He tells her her doctor really did get held up. That it's never as bad as it seems and one last line:

'You're much stronger than you think you are.'

Clark's right. You are. So am I. Never forget that.

April

The Late Shift

The Quickness of the Hand

*(This essay originally appeared on PseudoPod episode 328, "**The Suicide Witch**" by Vylar Kaftan, narrated by Rikki LaCoste on April 5th 2013)*

When I was a teenager, shortly before I was considering being a monk, I was a magician. Stage magic is one of those pure, holy arts that, at that point, everyone largely overlooked. Penn and Teller were just getting traction, Derren Brown was a few years off hitting big and the shadow of Paul bloody Daniels cast itself far and wide across the UK magical landscape, buying small towns, creating utterly- terrifying-in-retrospect kids TV shows and providing a crutch to lazy, half-assed comedians the country over.

Every single one of those things is true by the way. Go google 'Wizbit'. Be prepared to never sleep again. And no, I don't know:

A) What the Hell anyone involved in that show was thinking

or

B)Why he looked *grimy*.

Anyway, the thing I really dug about magic was twofold. Firstly - and anyone who has heard me speak, ever, already knows this - the best possible thing you can do is give me a live mic and a captive audience. I'm a talker. I am gregarious. Ebullient. Chatty. One universe over I was a stand-up comedian. In the universe past that I can only assume I got kicked out of the monastery for my vow of silence lasting under a minute

The second reason is elegance. Magic is suave, and not just in appearance either, although the top hat and tails is one hell of a work uniform. No, magic is elegant because it's simultaneously brash and absolutely calm. A magician will walk up to you, make something impossible happen and leave you with two gifts; the trick and the implication that, perhaps, Horatio really does need to do a little more reading. It's graceful, gentle, subversion. And at the heart of that subversion is misdirection.

It's a simple idea; you do something flashy and brilliant on your right whilst the obvious, easy, visible motion that actually powers the trick is taking place on your left. You put your audience where you want them to be or, if you're very good, you make them decide they want to be there so they don't realize you're controlling them. It's - weirdly - the same basic principle you see in a lot of martial arts; feint with the right so they move onto the left, fake one throw to land another, and my favourite from Aikido; move with your opponent and turn their own motion against them. Whichever version you choose it still ends up with your audience, or your opponent, or both, watching your right hand and trying to figure out where the dove came from.

It works socially too. There's a psychological trick an old friend told me which shows how it works. If you imagine a cloak covering you from head to toe, you'll walk through most crowds completely unnoticed. There's nothing odd about it, it's just a trick that makes you feel invisible, alters your posture and gait and in doing so, means other people forget to notice you.

My favourite one though, is the old story about an exercise some police departments like to run. They have, at a random time each year, a man come into a class and clean the windows. As the class finishes, the teacher stops them where they are and tells them all to write a description of the cleaner.

None of them are the same. Ever. And, the story goes, there's often someone who claims no one came in at all.

A similar study a few years ago involved a moment of Monty Python-esque absurdity. Subjects were set up to talk to someone in a university quad where this took place and, halfway through each conversation, a pair of workmen would walk between the two, carrying a door.

When they moved on, the person the subject was talking to had changed.

Not everyone noticed.

My point is this. We can all step outside the sphere of attention of everyone else on the planet pretty easily. Hell I'm 6'2 and have a shaved head most of the time which automatically puts me on the 'DON'T MAKE EYE CONTACT' list for some people. Its misdirection, just like magic, just like martial arts. Shifting the audience's, or the opponent's, attention to where you want it to be instead of where it is. Use it wisely. Have some fun.

Oh and is this your wallet?

Mosaic

*(This essay originally appeared on PseudoPod episode 329, "**Red Rubber Gloves**" by Christine Brooke-Rose, narrated by Kim Lakin-Smith on April 12th 2013)*

I used to live in a house that was slightly underground. It was a promenade, one of very few in the city, which meant it was shut off to traffic. This in turn meant every takeout place other than the one at the bottom of the road got frightened and confused by the street and taxi drivers tried to kill it with their brains every time they went past.

It also meant it was quiet.

So quiet there was a fox den somewhere in the bank across the street from the house. So quiet that, in the middle of winter, Marguerite once opened the front door and we saw an owl sitting in the tree in the front garden. It saw us and there was that moment of '…awkward…' inter-species communication and then it flew off. In silence.

We were lucky there for a couple of reasons, not the least of which was our neighbours who were shouty, if polite, on one side and wonderful on the other. Bev and Sam helped us out immensely and were cheerfully up front about the fact that whilst the area wasn't any sketchier than most student neighbourhoods it was a little sketchier than some. They had a menagerie of dogs and cats, every shape and size, and at least one of them had been rescued from the local drug dealers. As in; Bev saw the cat was in a state, took it in, kicked the door in at the drug dealer's place and told them the cat belonged to her now and if they had a problem so did SHE.

Like I say, very cool. Also pretty badass. And also that drug dealer house was somewhere nearby. I never had it confirmed, but I'm pretty sure the big place with the security cameras on every door and the 'CROSS THE ROAD. DO IT NOW' atmosphere was probably it.

We live our lives stacked on top of and side by side with people we never know and never will. But sometimes, we get a glimpse at their lives.

Here's another one; a few months after that we had a long weekend in Dublin. I love Dublin and it, as usual, did not disappoint. In the space of three days we got to hang out with my sister, her then boyfriend and his three kids, go see a Dead Can Dance concert (Neither one of us believes in a bucket list but seeing DCD again would officially be on Marguerite's list if she had one) and got charm-mugged into trying a specific restaurant.

Also? There was what is now referred to as *The Dublin Incident.*

So, the concert lets out after two encores and it's midnight. We're on the waterfront and our hotel is on Fleet Street (And yes I got a huge kick out of that, and, yes I'm fairly certain Marguerite picked it on purpose. She's lovely that way), just over an hour away. No problem, we figured, we'd walk, be faster than waiting for a taxi.

The hour passes, and we chat quite happily, all the while making our way through the cheerfully hammered Halloween throng. Turns out it was a little bit further out and by the time we got within twenty minutes of the hotel two things occurred to us; we hadn't eaten in about six hours and pretty much everywhere we could eat was closed.

Except.

One.

Like Bill Hicks once said, I'm not proud but I was hungry. So, in we went and had McDonalds and it was GLORIOUS. Salty, greasy glory stuffed to the nines with calories and at no point did we give a single, solitary damn. I was reminded of University, where every movie would be followed by dissecting it with friends Stuart, Helen and Karen over a Mcdonalds and a milkshake so thick you'd get a nosebleed trying to suck it up.

(An aside: Stuart, post-*Starship Troopers*, rolling a straw up and yelling 'Hey! Hey look! My milkshake is Xander!' and stabbing the straw into the cup still makes me laugh close to twenty years later.)

It was good. Almost…*too*…good. So we made a rule; McDonalds is acceptable outside the country, but inside, a big no-no. It's a good rule, works well and means that Sausage McBiscuits can legitimately happen whenever we're in the US.

Don't judge me.

All that was fun, but what stays with me is what we saw on the ride to the airport at *Oh My God* o'clock the day before. The bus left at about 4.30 from the town centre and its passengers consisted of Marguerite, me, three students who'd managed to miss every single other bus on the planet and a driver who you could almost hear mentally counting the money he was earning.

The only people on the streets were utility workers and prostitutes. Nottingham was all sodium light, empty streets and people starting their day whilst the night shift finished their own.

Years ago, walking along the promenade in Douglas, chatting to a couple of friends, a young woman came up to us. She was maybe a year or two older than the sacks of teenage hormones with vocal chords she was approaching. She muttered something and I said 'not today thanks' on autopilot because I'm British and then an old lady passing the other way yelled 'WHORE! YOU SHOULD BE ASHAMED!' and chased her off.

I've thought about that on and off for close to a decade and a half. Firstly because I was completely ignorant to what was going on, and also because it was an insight into another world, another life, the lens gears whirring as the universe focused on someone else for a second and they were having a much worse time than me. A view through a window, half obscured, a second of someone else's story.

Perhaps I was wrong earlier and Elbow were right. Everyone really IS here, we're just not all talking to each other. The choice to do so, the choice to reach out to help someone else or just observe their life from a distance is hugely difficult and whether or not it's the right thing to do is always changing. Do you step in and help or do you stand and watch? Which helps? Which hinders? What did you really see? The uncertainty behind it is true horror, the sense not of something massive brushing past you but of something, small, fragile and human. Something familiar and, possibly, horrifying. Or maybe just a pair of red rubber gloves.

Durden's People

*(This essay originally appeared on PseudoPod episode 330, Flash on the Borderlands XV: At Your Service! Featuring "**Last Waltz in Texas**" by Bryce Albertson, narrated by Jacquie Duckworth, "**Sterile**" by Christopher Tepedino, narrated by John Bell, and "**Meat**" by David Steffen, narrated by Josh Roseman on April 19th 2013)*

I've spent a good chunk of time in the service industry. It's an interesting place, especially in the UK where the class system always looks over you like a faintly disenchanted, bored schoolmaster. My first cleaning job was great, it was a couple of years ago providing holiday cover and working with the cheeriest person I've ever met. Nikki was fiercely smart, completely charming and utterly honest and we spent three hours a night cleaning the Government Ombudsman building in York. Which, it being York, was of course a faintly Hogwartsian mansion house complete with a dumb waiter and a ghost.

So, with my head all full of bad wiring from the last couple of years and my iPod full of MC Frontalot, I got on with the business of getting rid of other people's detritus. It was easy, and relaxing, and fun. I've had no luck with full time work these last couple of years and the voice that always whispers to you, the one that says you're unemployable, that you'll always be poor and broken and outside, that voice was getting louder. Nikki and her mammoth tea breaks and complete enthusiasm for everything, along with MC Frontalot of course, changed that and I'll always be grateful, both for the time off from the world and the friendship. And of course, the tea.

My second job was less successful. It was still fun but it was for a building supplies firm on the outskirts of York. They were all fine people, but there was one floor, where the sales execs worked where I felt myself…fade. These were all men, a good five years younger than me with all the stupidity that your late 20s knocks out still very much intact, and the scent of concrete and testosterone was gag-inducing. I wasn't a person when I cleared their bins; I was an extrusion of the building, a tool that moved. Useful meat.

That sense of invisibility evolved by the time I moved to Nottingham. 2012 was a fairly awful year for me professionally. So, when a cleaning job came up I jumped at it. The advantages were threefold; the work was part-time, the work was physically very demanding at a time when I desperately needed to lose weight and the work was cathartic. I welcomed the possibility of a job that A)Noticed me and B)Paid me the same decade I did the work.

The downside to it was twofold and I'm not super proud of one of those things. The understandable downside was the hours; at one point my day started at noon, finished at 10pm and took in roughly eight hours of cleaning in four different buildings in two different towns. I shifted a good chunk of weight and I've kept it off but that was as much down to having no time to eat anything real as the actual exercise.

The second reason speaks entirely to the sort of entitlement I'm terrified of relaxing into. I have a Bachelors in English and History, a Masters in Contemporary English Literature and I've worked for multiple publications for multiple years and hit every single target I've been pointed at.

And my reward for this? A pair of office jobs so traumatic I had trouble setting foot in an office for a while, and to spend my evenings cleaning up after people who think bins are magical portals to infinite realms of waste disposal and who don't understand hole punches.

On my bad nights it didn't feel like a job, it felt like servitude, and that's something the UK is still far more in love with than it wants to admit. We like to not acknowledge the person behind the counter and we love to conflate the word 'staff' with the word 'servant' and that's especially true of the genre live event community. Around the same time Conan Doyle's estate finally declassify The Giant Rat of Sumatra case I'll write about the things that have happened when I've volunteered at 'cons. No one does the class system like the geeks, kids. Usually whilst loudly proclaiming how liberal and accepting they are. To the same people they've had the conversation with for decades.

So here's a thought; don't do that. Say hi to the people behind the counter, buy your cleaner some bloody chocolates at Christmas and if you can, take a service job. The world turns a little smoother because of these people and, like Tyler Durden once said, they're everywhere. And they see you, even when you don't see them.

The Ninth Skeleton

*(This essay originally appeared on PseudoPod episode 331, "**The Ninth Skeleton**" by Clark Ashton-Smith, narrated by Corson Bremer on April 16th 2013)*

I always like stories like this. There's a lot of mileage in stories where the main character runs off the edge of the world, and takes a while to notice. *Cell Call* by Marc Laidlaw a little while back does exactly the same thing.

What makes this one different, and what, I suspect, may be annoying some of you right now is the lack of explanation. There's no real context for what the narrator sees and that could in some cases be viewed as a weakness. It probably is. Here though I think it's a strength, the ambiguity shaping the horror rather than limiting it. *Picnic at Hanging Rock*, the 1967 novel by Joan Lindsay and later the movie directed by Peter Weir is very similar. In that, a group of school girls go on an expedition to a nearby geological formation, Hanging Rock. There, several climb to the top and, in a dream like sequence, walk into a crevice in the rock and vanish. The frantic - and partially successful - search for them is chilling not because we get answers but because we get incomplete ones as we do here. Something is wrong at Hanging Rock, something is wrong with the location the narrator visits. I especially admire the chilling implication that Guinevere as the ninth skeleton suggests there may be something bad in her immediate future. I hope that's not the case, and the fact that the story can elicit that hope in me proves that there's something there. Ambiguity, the half-glimpsed shape that passes you by, the moment where you realize the boundary between fantasy and reality is several miles behind you and the road may not be there anymore. Horror lives in the same place as discovery a lot of the time and the difference is sometimes very small and the line is sometimes very easy to cross. The narrator here got lucky, most don't.

May

Travellers and Traffic

GRAVEL'S GAME

*(This essay originally appeared on PseudoPod episode 332, "**Willow Tests Well**" by Nick Mamatas, narrated by Julie Hoverton on May 3rd 2013)*

William Gravel is one of Warren Ellis' best bastards. Gravel is a disgraced SAS combat magician who is currently on deniable ops, meaning he can be put into any given situation, has free reign to solve it how he sees fit and no one will be especially bothered if he dies. This suits Gravel just fine, especially as he gets to spend a lot of time in America. In one particular issue, Gravel is given some good-natured shit by an old friend about England and responds by implying, heavily, that America is a centuries-long sociological experiment being conducted by the Crown and they're really rather pleased with how it's going.

Similarly, *Desolation Jones*, also created by Ellis, posits that LA, already a notional city formed from a network of towns and roads rather than an actual one, is an open prison for disgraced or broken spies. You get dumped in LA when you're no use to anyone else and you can do whatever you want to whoever you want inside the city, as long as you're not caught. Or try to leave.

Closer to home; a friend of a friend was, purportedly, in final stages of selection for MI5 when we were at University. Ian was massively smart, relentlessly hard working and completely charming. He was also an avid UFOlogist and just a teeny bit ambiguous which means he was either an epic bullshitter or he was legitimately on final selection. I leave the choice up to you, and simply point out that when he was initially selected for interview, he told me that the letter came with a series of black and white photos of his father and he, out at a coffee shop. The message was simple; play nice, we're watching.

Good story. The sort that doesn't matter if it's true or not.

That idea, the weaponization of sociopathy, is something that lies at the heart of a lot of great espionage fiction, not to mention field work. It goes back to Nixon and the mad bomber approach. It's not pleasant, by any stretch of the imagination, but as a bargaining tool it can be brutally effective. The only problem is if you're the crazy guy in the room, you have to always be the crazy guy in the room from that point on. It's a role you can choose to play but one which it's very difficult to choose NOT to.

Now imagine being conditioned to be that way. Pushed and threatened and enabled in a way which drives you forward through events which break other people but only ever make you stronger. Imagine how tired you must feel. Imagine how tired Willow is. Monsters need sleep too.

Last of the Gunslingers

*(This essay originally appeared on PseudoPod episode 333, "**Gig Marks**" by Ed Ferrara, narrated by Patrick Bazile on May 10th 2013)*

There's a term from the McCarthy era that I always loved; fellow travellers. Obviously not in the way McCarthy intended but there's some kinship to the term I've always found endearing. Last summer, when I was out in the US we'd often be driving back from somewhere late at night and there was one time especially, coming down the mountain from Marguerite's grandparents' house that really struck me. That road is MASSIVE fun by the way, on a clear day you can hurl a car around it going up a good two to three hundred plus feet without having to slow down on anything other than the occasional curves. On a bad day, you get stuck behind a tractor or a truck or someone who finds the road being invisible ahead of them frightening. Either way it's a beautiful ride, but if you're lucky, it's a FUN one too.

Coming down tends to be slightly different, because you get traffic, especially at weekends, coming back from Santa Cruz. So, we'd spend a good couple of hours at a time driving down the mountain in rolling traffic, chatting, looking at the countryside and looking at the people around us. The other pockets of humanity, the other snatches of music that you hear as you pass by. A thousand stories in close formation, all heading in the same direction but all unique.

There was this one guy, hand to God, I'll even see if I've still got the photo and link it, who was driving a van marked BIGFOOT RESCUE PATROL.

It had a cage on the back.

He was dressed like a park ranger.

Questions filled my mind, does this guy work alone? Has he ever caught one? Who pays him? Flashes of someone else's story, passing you by on the road.

That's how I feel about pro wrestlers, they're fellow travellers. Anyone who tells you pro wrestlers don't work harder than very nearly every other entertainer on the planet is an idiot, these are people who drive themselves around the world for years at a time, making a living not just through fighting, but through staged, intricately choreographed fights. Often more than once a day. The arts and the martial arts, all rolled into one, usually flamboyant and always, underneath the adrenalin, so very tired. Some of my closest friends are working or have worked in the industry, you may even have seen them. They work harder than anyone I know for less than almost anyone I know and if I wanted to, I could launch into a lengthy potted lecture about the history of the industry and everything that's been perpetrated against its stars, often by themselves, more often by the industry itself.

Instead, I'll say this. These people are wandering entertainers who make their living not just with their muscles but with their brains. They're one step to the side of circus culture, one step to the other side of boxing culture and every inch artists, just like writers, artists and composers. And just like us they have their stories and their traditions and this one, for me, sits perfectly in that pantheon.

So to my friends in the business, Matt Wallace and Kat Waters, I salute you. Likewise the mixed martial artists I know, the incredible Julie Kedzie, Nathan Leverton and the rest. All artists deserve respect but the ones whose medium is heel heat and cheap pops, arm bars and teep kicks, blood and sweat? They EARN it.

Island Zen

*(This essay originally appeared on PseudoPod episode 334, "**The Curse of the Mummy**" by Andre Harden, narrated by Emily Smith on May 17th 2013)*

I'm from a very small place, and when you come from somewhere like that, everywhere seems massive. Marguerite still, from time to time, looks at me with a combination of amusement and pity when I try and call the tower blocks round the back of the house skyscrapers with a straight face.

It's all a matter of scale. When I was growing up, it was a HUGE deal going to the island's capital because Douglas was half an hour away. **BY CAR!**

Similarly, there are places on the other side of the island that I visited precisely twice in 18 years. Why? Because when you live somewhere that you can walk from one end of to the other in a day, your sense of scale adjusts accordingly.

Everything's possible but nothing's achievable because whilst Ian Malcolm was right and life finds a way, life also finds a way of getting IN the way. The sense of frustration, of life passing you by, in places like that is so thick you could roll it in chocolate and call it a snow cone. It's worse in the states, weirdly. Last year, driving to San Diego, we saw towns that were literally convenience stores, truck stops and that's it. Places defined by the need to stop on the way somewhere else.

There's an insidious kind of desperation that creeps in, in places like that. The kind that erodes your will with every passing day and every passing truck. You start thinking about what the rest of the world is like and when you find out, when the rest of the world comes knocking at your door, you take anything you can damn well get. Some of my favourite horror stories start in places like this, some of them you've heard here, some of them you may have seen. Not so much the restaurant at the end of the universe as the diner at the end of the line. Endless times call for desperate measures and what's the difference between a mummy and a key filled with the blood of Christ, or a tape that kills you seven days after you watch it?

Easy.

The difference is whoever guards the box, holds the key, and watches the tape. Curses can be borne, hard choices made. Heroes forged in towns that are truck stops, gas stations and nothing else. And even if we only ever see them as we pass by on the way to somewhere bigger, they still count.

Johnny Bob and the Faustettes

*(This essay originally appeared on PseudoPod episode 335, "**Charlie Harmer's Day Off**" by Brendan Detzner, narrated by Eric Luke on May 24th 2013)*

Here's you. Here's what we want. Here's what you have. That's what we take.

That simple, Faustian deal is wrapped up in the one thing everyone wants and everyone always has wanted; release. A day off. A chance to not be you, not be nice, not be there. Step out of the rat race and trip up a few people on the way out if you want to. It's the same instinct that makes the *GTA* and *Saints Row* games so popular and it's a very healthy one. Everyone needs to blow off some steam and whilst the method here is wrong, the wish is right.

Life goes past pretty quickly as Ferris once said. What he didn't say was how hard it is. We live next to so much that sometimes we find ourselves living IN almost, a thinly veiled fantasy where things are different, where you save money and leave town like last week, where the woman of your dreams sees the man of her dreams when she looks at you, or vice versa. Where things are different and different by your hand and you're recognised and lauded for that.

But that almost never happens. And sometimes the music isn't loud enough and all you can see is the years in the store, the years spent helping other people and the years spent waiting for other people to help you. I've worked retail, and niche retail at that, I know what it feels like to be waiting for your life to change and to realize, but not quite see, that that's the whole problem. You change or wait for the change to come to you and the change here is truly horrible. The abject loss of control on one side, balanced against a taste of life and the consequences of that on the other. No wonder Charlie leaves. The price is paid by both sides, after all. That simple, primal, awful deal coupled with a slick, faceless, ghostly middle manager. That's a image that's uniquely horrible and not one I'll soon forget.

There's always a price. Someone always pays. It's usually you. Make sure you can cover the cheque.

The Abyss

*(This essay originally appeared on PseudoPod episode 336, "**The Abyss**" by Leonid Andreyev, narrated by Tanja Milojevic on May 31st 2013)*

The Abyss has on-ramps. A lot of them are signposted. A lot more aren't. Sometimes you don't know when you're in there, until you've been there a while, the walls leaning across to touch each other far, far above your head. Other times, when you're faced with something that's awful, and will always be awful, always be happening, you run headlong for it because that's the only place you can go.

Why leave?

The Abyss looks exactly like everywhere else a lot of the time, just with the shades drawn, the volume turned down. The Abyss has friends and family in it, shops, places you know, things you like to do. Everything's down there and that's the thing no one ever remembers. The Abyss isn't cold and dark and lonely. The Abyss is where everyone lives, and the fact everyone is down there means EVERYONE is down there.

Why leave?

The Abyss is forgiving. The Abyss loves you and knows all your faults and accepts them, because your faults are what brought you there and keep you there and who's perfect? Who doesn't deserve to live in the Abyss?

Why leave?

The Abyss is protective. When you flee to the abyss to escape the world, and you will, then the abyss will put itself between you and harm. The world will be a little dimmer, you'll walk slower, your shoulders will hunch more but that's a small price to pay for protection. That's a small price to pay for living somewhere that knows you and accepts you and somehow still loves you isn't it?

Why leave?

The Abyss is as old as you are. The Abyss has been there for as long as you have, waiting for you because the abyss, unlike heaven, is open even at Christmas. The Abyss will wait for you and when you want to go there, the abyss will be there, waiting. It's the arm around your shoulder, the bottle, the drug, the food, the orgasm that takes the back of your head off. It's release.

Why leave?

The Abyss is your home.

Why leave?

The world outside the abyss wants to do nothing but harm you.

Why leave?

The only thing out there is the trauma that you were fleeing from. Do you want to look? Do you want to know what's out there for you? Waiting?

WHY LEAVE?

Because a life lived turned away from horror is no life at all. Because the healing process is one we resent because it takes so long and one we love because it eventually ends. Because the abyss is filled with ghosts and as long as you know you can't stay, you know you're not one of them. Death, depression, addiction, whatever drives you there doesn't matter. What matters is you climb out. We'll all be cheering you on.

June

Gravity

Spectrum is Green

*(This essay originally appeared on PseudoPod episode 338, "**Beware the Jabberwock, My Son**" by Dixon Chance, narrated by Kevin Hayes on June 14th, 2013)*

In the UK, the name Gerry Anderson is mentioned in the same breath as *Doctor Who* or the Muppets would be in the US. Anderson, and his then-wife Sylvia, perfected a flotilla of science-fiction action adventure puppet TV shows that ran for years in the UK and had a half-life measured in decades. One that's still active.

These shows ran the gamut from jaunty and child-orientated science fiction with *Fireball XL5* to something altogether darker and more mature with *Captain Scarlet*. That show followed the members of SPECTRUM, a team of elite soldiers and scientists based on a flying aircraft carrier (Yep) who battled the Mysterons, a Martian race able to possess organic matter and repair even the most hellacious damage. Captain Scarlet, the lead, was turned by the Mysterons in the pilot and technically killed. However, he broke the conditioning and returned to fight them as an agent of SPECTRUM. Which, when you think about it, must have royally pissed off every non alien-enhanced, mortal SPECTRUM agent. I can picture the briefings now

'What do you mean I have to go into the nuclear reactor? Send Scarlet! Is this because I'm Captain Puce?! It's because I'm Captain Puce isn't it?!'

Of course my brain then goes to the idea of Colonel White (Yes I know) engineering similar 'accidents' for the rest of his staff. But, then again, my brain also imagines the other Anderson series *Thunderbirds* as being one step away from a story about a global coup and at one point worked out how to remake *Charlie's Angels* as the sort of cold, eccentric spy fiction that Warren Ellis excels at.

Picture *Girls* crossed with *Agents of SHIELD* and the *Guardians of the Galaxy* soundtrack.

Your move, Hollywood.

While we're waiting, I should say I mention the Andersons here because of a lesser known part of their work. *Doppelganger* was co-written by them and followed an astronaut recuperating after a long duration mission. He slowly came to realize that he's not landed on Earth, but rather its identical, reversed twin. An identical-sized planet orbiting the Sun at the same distance and speed as the Earth, but in the other direction and therefore undetectable. The premise is wonderfully goofy but it pays off because of two things; firstly the absolutely straight way it's played and secondly the ending. Decades after the story, one of the main characters is in a nursing home. He sees his reflection and, convinced it's the counter Earth, hurls himself forward smashing through the mirror. It's an intense, nasty scene that aired in the middle of the day over here and, along with a couple of other movies like it, has stayed with me ever since.

The fascination with what's on the other side of the mirror is easy to understand. After all it's both us and not us, a warts-and-all portrayal of yourself but flipped in such a way that it seems new and different. It's where the roots of narcissism and introspection lie, after all the phrase is 'Take a long hard look at yourself.'

But it gets really interesting, and disturbing, when what's on the other side of the mirror looks back.

The idea of the mirror as a trap, as something that can hunt you is fascinating, and used to chilling effect both in the movie and this story. I'm reminded of several of the stories in *Looking for Jake*, the China Mieville anthology that play with something very similar. A reflection. A dark twin. A doppelganger. The room on the other side of the mirror is never empty and sometimes, as here, the mirror is actually a door. Sometimes it's a door that leads to understanding and self-knowledge, even if that self-knowledge is just that you need a haircut. Sometimes it's a door that only opens one way. Sometimes you'll wish it was.

Smells Like Teen Idiot

*(This essay originally appeared on PseudoPod episode 339, "**The End-of-the-World Pool**" by Scott M. Roberts, narrated by Mark E. Phair on June 21st 2013)*

There's a quote about existentialism that I rather like:

"The archetypal example is the experience one has when standing on a cliff where one not only fears falling off it, but also dreads the possibility of throwing oneself off. In this experience that "nothing is holding me back", one senses the lack of anything that predetermines you to either throw yourself off or to stand still, and one experiences one's own freedom."

That didn't occur to me, close to 20 years ago, when I was hanging off the side of a cliff with nothing but the rapidly severing tufts of grass in my hand to stop me from falling 15 or so feet down onto a beach made of rocks and serious injury. Nothing, to be honest, was going through my mind at that exact point other than a much less polite version of 'I think I may have made a mistake.'

I was 18 you see, and a moron. My friend Pete was late with the chips and the steps were entirely too far away so I thought I'd climb the rock to get back up to the road where the chip shop was and…anyway. I did 15 feet, maybe 20, free climbing with the enthusiasm born of lots of nice handholds and absolutely no sense of mortality, both of which evaporated at about the same time.

They were replaced by gravity and adrenalin-soaked terror. I hauled myself up the last eight feet, got to the top of the road, and Pete was just leaving the chip shop. I like to think he looked at me, bedraggled and covered in mud and grass and just went '…what?' but this is the man who once went for a drink, had another, then another, then got on a train, then it was night time and he was tired so he slept under a hedge, woke up and called the villa he was staying at in France to come and get him so really anything's possible.

My point is this; children are bulletproof right up until the point they realize they aren't.

Then, the hormonal motorcycle of adolescence is parked outside and the keys are in it and they're only going to take it for a spin for a few years, I mean how hard can it be? Cue varying amounts of booze, drugs, sex, a little violence for some, magnificently outrageous music they'll return to like an old battered teddy bear in their 30s and maybe the odd tattoo. At the end of the process they look like an adult but are in fact, a sentient scream of terror at just how HUGE AND COMPLICATED EVERYTHING IS NOW.

But underneath it all, they're still bound to the people they grew up with by chains of iron. You never forget your first bully, your first crush, your first best friend or any of the ones that come after that. They get distant, certainly, but they're always there and so are the people who stood by you. The kids riding the other motorbikes in parallel with yours, screaming and laughing with the exuberant terror of getting away with this stuff even as every second brings getting caught hurtling closer. These are the people you love, and hate, and fight and miss. The people who, when they ring in the middle of the night for a favour, know you've agreed before they start talking and that they'd do the same for you. These are the people who've saved your life and whose lives you'll save. These are your friends. Trust them, they trust you and regardless of who's bleeding at the end of the day, you'll always come home.

And do me a favour? WAIT for the bloody chips.

'How frail the human heart must be - a mirrored pool of thought.'
Sylvia Plath

Neighbourhood Watching

*(This essay originally appeared on PseudoPod episode 340, "**Neighbourhood Watch**" by Greg Egan, narrated by Ron Jon Newton on June 28th 2013)*

There's a shot in *Blue Velvet*, the David Lynch movie, which is one of the few times I genuinely get Lynch's viewpoint. Don't get me wrong I like a good deal of his stuff, and one day look forward to visiting the parallel universe where *Mulholland Drive* is on its tenth season but a lot of the time I find myself admiring his work rather than liking it.

This one shot is different though. The camera tracks down past a Norman Rockwell full-blown Americana house, down into the lawn and reveals a horrific, squirming mass of insects. The metaphor's brilliant; nothing's perfect under the surface, everywhere has a dark side. It's Lynch as cryptkeeper, smiling and holding the curtain back however loudly you scream for him to let it drop.

It's also, by and large, true. I grew up in the archetypal small town and that meant I grew up in the same soup of rumour and innuendo that everyone does. I could, with a little effort, tell you the bus stop that children who didn't want to go home would sleep in. I could with a little more effort point out the boy who was said to have almost died when he poured petrol over himself and set it alight to see what would happen. And I could with no effort at all point you at the kid who, so the story goes, was caught licking melted chocolate off his dog's stomach. A squirming, chthonic morass of innuendo and rumour and in the middle of it, the one thing worse than that; the truth. It didn't matter if any of these stories were true, it mattered that they got repeated and that gave them life and that life gave them power. So you learned the places to not go, the things to not ask. You learned to be quiet, learned to be loud because children are expected to be and most of all you learned not to talk about it. Because if you talked about it, if you looked the monsters all around you in the eye, then that meant they were real. Worse still, you'd have to do something about them before they decided to do something about you.

That perverse level of emotional blindness is a shield we all have. If you can't see it then it isn't happening and if it isn't happening it can't hurt you. It's also crap, by the way. If something bad is happening, acknowledge it because that gives it boundaries and once that's done? Start doing something about it, even if what you have to do is incredibly difficult. Because once you've seen the elephant in the room, you can never unsee it.

I just finished reading *Joyland*, the new Stephen King, and there's a line in there that really jumped out at me. At one point, one of the characters turns to another and says

'Don't worry, it won't be the last good time.'

That fear, that the price you pay for confronting something is the total surgical removal of happiness, is completely understandable, almost universal and a chain that binds us all to the now. There's always one more good time, or the memory of one more good time and even if there isn't for you, there always will be for someone else. The trick is to accept that as a win too. Because the moment you do, the monsters you're facing have no power and are dragged, screaming, out into the light that will burn them away.

'... look down on the enemy,
and take up your attitude on slightly higher places.
Musashi Miyamoto, The Book of Five Rings

July

The Unknown

The Monsters Have Bought Property On Maple Street

*(This essay originally appeared on PseudoPod episode 341, "**Immortal L.A.**" by Eric Czuczleger, narrated by Joe Calarco on July 5th 2013)*

I remember, back in the heady, vibrant and now surprisingly badly dressed days of the 1990s, the original plan for the third *Blade* movie was that it would be a soft takeover. Gradually the vampires would just stop hiding and they'd have so many vessels in so many places that it really didn't matter what anyone did, so…we rolled over. Society began a slow collapse into being nothing but a feedbag because the marketing said that's what the SEXY people wanted.

That's an awfully cynical way of looking at things, I'll grant you, and the movie ended up going in a different direction. But that idea, of the vampire as this all-seeing, all-knowing omnipresent figure has actually been on the wane for a while now. And no I'm not going to make the obvious joke about the obvious movie franchise because it's over now. The last film's out, the last book's out and we all need to move on with our lives and find something else as a benchmark of suck.

The fall of the vampire started before those books that shall not be named and it's continuing unabated. I just read the first volume of Max Brooks' *The Extinction Parade*, which he's adapting for comics for Avatar Press. There, the vampire, the fictional figure that once soared across the night time of a thousand terrified children reading Dracula before they understood it, is…a member of the 1%. The idle and immortal rich, so bored that they treat a zombie outbreak like a tourist attraction. Now that doesn't go so well for them, but the fact remains, the vampire is no longer a paragon of undead animals, no longer a towering figure of horror and fear.

And I'd argue, all the more interesting for it.

Look at Justin Cronin's *The Fall,* Guillermo Del Toro and Chuck Hogan's *The Strain* series or Greg Stolze's *Enzymes,* broadcast here a while back. All of them, to say nothing of *Supernatural* or *True Blood,* look at vampires as either the people on the other side of the street or the people on the other side of the bar. Majesty is replaced with mundanity but the horror, believe me, is still there.

The fear of the alien, the other, is one of the places where horror, current affairs and thrillers connect. The thing horror brings to the table that any amount of Jack Bauer table-thumping doesn't, is this; horror shows us just how terrified, just how flawed the monsters are. They still have to put their pants on one leg at a time and, in the case of vampires, have to face not only the possibility but the certainty of another night, another hunger, another death. Even if they choose not to, then the choices are corpse blood, animal blood or madness, starvation and death. Or, if they're lucky enough to live in New York and own a copy of the Shambling Guide, at the very least a good restaurant recommendation.

The monsters are already here, they've been here for years and just as we're tormented by the fear of them, they're tormented by the memory of what they used to be. That's the unifying thread that runs through these stories. Just because you live in the big city doesn't mean you're a success. Just because you're a vampire doesn't mean you have the answers. It just means you have to work harder to answer some different, tougher questions.

And that sounds like the basis to some good fiction doesn't it?

'we know how many foot taps it takes to make me appear. Wonderful.'
Malkavian, Vampire: The Masquerade: Bloodlines

Something More

*(This essay originally appeared on PseudoPod episode 342, "**Riding Atlas**" by Ferrett Steinmetz, narrated by Chris Reynaga on July 12th 2013)*

The need to be part of something bigger lies at the heart of almost every area of society. Whether it's supporting a team, or a comic company, joining a religion, being part of a family, we all want something which takes us out of ourselves. Sometimes it's social interaction and everything that comes with it, sometimes it's a solitary escape into a book, or a game or a film. Trust me, I know how fast that screen expands and sucks you in and I know how many times in your life you desperately need it to.

Also, sometimes your brain colours monochrome images. The first TV I had, which I'm fairly certain was the first TV my parents had, was made out of Bakelite and sputnik. It was tiny. It was this awesome little black and white TV that weighed about the same amount as a quarterback and when we moved into the heady world of the colour Cathode ray, I inherited it. I always remember playing with the tuning dial to get a picture.

A tuning dial.

I'm mildly amazed the thing didn't have valves.

It took a while to get the picture just right and once it was there, feeling myself just…settle. Like breathing out into an expanding room.

Knight Rider was when I noticed it. That opening shot of the desert and the car knifing out of it, the narration 'This is the story of a man who does not exist.' and the driving and oh so '80s electronic soundtrack grabbed me by the brain and refused to let go.

And the thing is, after 30 seconds, it all turned colour. The really weird thing is the moment I noticed I was seeing it in colour, it went back to monochrome.

We reach out for something bigger all the time and the only thing that terrifies us more than missing it is reaching it, noticing and having it snatched away. We're changed by the journey, every single time but that change is nothing compared to the destination. We touch something bigger than ourselves and it destroys and rebuilds us into someone completely different. It's a crucible, a dividing line and once it's stopped there will always be the version of you that came out and the version of you that didn't. For some people that's a process that will take years to make peace with. Look at the problems many Apollo astronauts had when they reached not just the edge of their career path but the edge of astronautical history and capability.

We all know how to lose.

But how do we win?

The Apollo astronauts struggled, and some still do. But for some it's a blessing, a chance to start over with nothing because that would be easier than rebuilding with what they had. Escape, survival, destruction and victory all combined on the absolute edge of human experience. Nothing's the same once you've been part of something bigger. And none of us would have it any other way.

'... as they fashioned out of mud, the dragon, Ogdru Jahad.'
Hellboy

Tea and Crumpets At The End Of The World

*(This essay originally appeared on PseudoPod episode 343, "**Magdala Amygdala**" by Lucy Snyder, narrated by the late, much missed Eugie Foster on July 19th 2013)*

There's no such thing as totality, everything moves at a different speed and that means that the idea of any event being absolute, any change to the world being total is a misnomer. Look at disease vectors, how diseases can be tracked from their initial point of contact with humanity out through transportation networks, airports and then...then things get granular and complex and vague. That's where the apocalypse's edge blurs, where it starts to fuse with normal life in a way which a lot of authors overlook and really shouldn't. Because that's where things get interesting.

Not to mention dangerous.

Years ago, the Foot and Mouth outbreak in the UK devastated farming communities and led to scenes that would actually influence apocalyptic fiction. Both *Children of Men* and *28 Weeks Later* took cues from the horrific spread and scale of the outbreak especially the sight of countless cows, euthanized and burned in mass graves

I remember going on holiday to the Lake District and whatever road you took, sooner or later, your car would have to drive through anti-septic troughs. Even places off the mainland were hit, with the Isle of Man government deciding to not run the TT motorbike races that year in order to protect the island's cow population. In economic terms, that's like cancelling the Kentucky Derby or telling a Vegas casino it has to close over the 4th of July weekend. The effect was devastating but the effect of the disease getting onto a tiny, enclosed farming community would have been catastrophic.

I was working in the comic store at the time and one of our regular customers, a very nice chap called Glen, was with what was then the Ministry of Agriculture and Fisheries or MAF. Glen was a field scientist, and he was third string. That meant he went after the kill team, after the clean-up team and made sure everything was safe to let animals back in. I always remember him telling me they were terrified that the disease would jump to not just pigs but wild boars. Because no one had any idea how many there were in the country or where they were.

On the one hand I find something lovely in that. The idea that an entire animal can still slip through the cracks carries just a whisper of the old Woods to it, don't you think? The forest that once covered the country is still there if you know where to look and some species know far better than we do.

On the other hand, the country's ecology and economy could have been devastated by a single animal. And almost no one ever knew.

That's the bleeding edge of the soft apocalypse, the moment where everything can change and no one will see until it's happened. It's the moment in *Shaun of the Dead* where Shaun sees the tramp attacking the seagulls in the park, the first time the words 'martial law' are mentioned in the movie version of *World War Z*, Arthur Leander's death in the opening pages of Hilary St John Mandel's frankly staggering *Station Eleven*. Everything's already changed, you just don't know it yet. In fact, *Shaun*'s a perfect example of the soft apocalypse (And, because this is how nice I am, what follows are spoilers for a movie that's over a decade old).

The end of *Shaun*, where the zombie outbreak is contained and undead Ed is chained up in the shed is exactly the same thematic ground as St John Mandel and Brooks cover. The world doesn't end, because it's too big, it's too complex. It just changes and in the case of Shaun, society wraps the new underclass up in the blanket of polite acceptance and no eye contact and gives them crappy shift work. The not-quite-human are treated as not-quite-human but never confronted on that fact, because to do so would be to shatter the polite societal lie, the gossamer threads that hold everything in place. The world doesn't end, it just scars over again and the people affected learn to survive as best they can. Nine times out of ten, they don't rock the boat either because whilst the apocalypse is soft, there's always the fear of that changing. The world won't end, but it knows how. And so do the wild boar.

Meaningful Exchanges of Blows

*(This essay originally appeared on PseudoPod episode 344, "**The Pit**" by Joe R. Lansdale, narrated by John Bell on July 26th 2013)*

And now, like they say, for something completely different.

There are, I count, six different types of horror here. The first is the horror of the dogfight. Animal cruelty is one of my lines; you do anything to your animals, or anyone else's animals? We're done. Not just personally either, rapper DMX, a man who for a brief shining moment in the late '90s looked like a credible force in both rap and action cinema, and who styled himself on his pitbulls? Multiple arrests for animal cruelty.

Where my dogs at?

Loving homes where they're not treated like crap, asshole.

The second level of horror is far more elemental and springs from both the size of the dog in the fight and the fight left in the dog. We slow down. We are all, in the end, outlasted by entropy. You come out swinging, you score some good hits, you maybe even put it on its ass but entropy is always there, always beats the count and in the end, will, always break everything apart. Entropy is the undefeated world champion and always will be because its corner man is mortality. We get old. We get slow. No one ever retires when they should, especially if they're fighters.

Let's digress for a moment; I'm a Mixed Martial Arts fan. Not the chest pounding JUST BLEED dudebro school of MMA fandom by any means but the sort that believes it's a genuinely exciting sport and a fascinating, occasionally tedious, fusion of fighting styles. You want me to, I will hold forth about the relative merits of *Pride FC* over the *UFC*, I will talk at length about why *The Ultimate Fighter*, with some exceptions, is one of the greatest televisual crimes ever perpetrated in America and believe me I will evangelize about *Invicta FC*, the only all-female MMA promotion until the cows come home. I like martial arts. I like mixed martial arts and, inevitably, there are fighters who I'm an active fan of.

Two examples from that pack; Frank Mir and Stephen Bonnar. Mir, who is arguably the most laconic man in MMA, was UFC world champion at a relatively young age and then invalided out for an extended period due to a knee injury. He was treated abysmally by the promotion on his return and was eventually fed to former pro wrestler Brock Lesnar as a show fight. Against all expectations, Mir demolished his opponent in the first round. Since then, he's had a yoyo couple of years landing massive wins and massive defeats, more of the latter than the former. He is, definitively, in the later years of his career and is starting to head to the point where he needs to retire. Hopefully he will.

Stephen Bonnar, the man who placed second in the original season of the *Ultimate Fighter*, recently unretired for reasons almost as depressing as the circumstances of his retirement. Bonnar's last match was taken on short notice against then undefeated middleweight champion Anderson Silva. Silva is an astounding athlete, a martial artist with an emphasis on artist and a man who seems to move at a different speed to both his opponent and reality. Predictably, he dismantled Bonnar. However, Bonnar left the sport on his metaphorical shield and with a mind-set summed up by his final walkout t-shirt that read WE STEP UP.

What it should have read on the back is, BUT WE FAIL OUR UNEXPECTED DRUG TESTS.

Bonnar tested high for Performance Enhancing Drugs. And still lost. Legacy and career, all shot for one last chance at glory and a very finite pay check.

Entropy, in the end outpunches us all. But the secret, that neither the dogs nor the humans here are allowed to realize, is that throwing the towel in is actually a victory. Everyone's dying, slowly. Some of us are more prepared to mitigate that and work with it than others.

Then there's the subjugation of religion to violence. Which speaks to the same desire to touch something bigger as Ferrett Steinmetz's *Riding Atlas* which we talked about earlier in this chapter. The line in *Fight Club* about wanting to destroy something beautiful could just as easily be about wanting to see something beautiful destroyed and that's definitely an aspect of the 'worship' we see here. Voyeurs, aren't we all? As Eric Draven never quite said. It's the reason why people stop and watch arguments in the street or as happened this month, take pictures of a millionaire physically assaulting his wife on their camera phones instead of breaking it up. We want to be part of something great and if we can't be part of it we can at least stand by and watch it happen and say we were there. Thou shalt not kill becomes thou shalt place your bets and around we go.

Then there's the racism, hard coded into language to the point where it's almost part of the landscape. That's a very subtle choice on Lansdale's part and, like all good martial arts moves, it achieves two different things at once. The first is to highlight exactly how grotesquely hypocritical the 'church' is, how the pit fight is just an excuse to watch people die, preferably black people and if not black people now, black people eventually.

The second is to make you accept it.

There's so much else here, so much to be repulsed and fascinated by that it's possible to focus past the language, to focus past that word. When you do, when you realize what you've been letting happen in front of your eyes, that's truly horrific in a way nothing else in the story is.

Then there's the sexism, and the misogyny that goes with it. For a start the simple fact this is an entirely male gathering says everything you need to know about how they view women. There's the twisted decency of this 'not being for them' and the nasty, wild-eyed bloodlust of men behaving badly that echoes around the world every Friday night. This is men at their most feral; unbound, brutal, revelling in the war we've been conditioned to believe is the only thing there is for us.

But it's the freedom that stays with you. The memory one fighter has of his wife and how much he hated her. The simple fact that fighting to the death against a friend is more preferable than returning to her. The RELIEF that he doesn't have to, whatever happens. That's nihilistic in a way almost no fiction manages because almost no fiction is brave, or mad, enough to try. Except this.

Then there's the violence.

I'm tremendously lucky in this regard, I've only ever sparred in Judo and my brief foray into Thai Boxing finished before I was even safe enough to spar at semi-contact levels. That being said, the thing no one tells you about grappling forms is there's no such thing as semi-contact. You will be thrown onto your back, you will be picked up and hit very hard with the ground, you will be choked and have your joints extended and leave every session with a headache until you stop being stupid and tuck your damn chin when you land. Judo's the hardest thing I've ever done and at no point was anyone actively punching me. Also, at no point was I actively absent. That's the thing no one tells you about fighting, you're still you, still in your head and whilst it turns off higher brain functions pretty fast it doesn't turn off everything. You feel the pain, you feel the sensation of being moved around with hostile intent, your chest burning, your limbs aching.

Add bruises and blood.

Add the crack of your bones breaking.

Add the screams and taunts of a crowd who just want you to die, or kill and aren't fussy how or which.

Add the constant, frantic physical math as you work out if the damage that punch will do you is smaller than the damage it will do him.

Add the fact that whatever happens you know one of you is not leaving the pit and the other may be permanently mauled by the fight.

No escape.

No hope.

No chance.

Unless you fight.

And if you fight you destroy yourself physically and psychologically whatever happens, win or lose. Horror. Monolithic horror that's the only thing you can see and the only thing left and even that won't help you.

No the only thing that will do that is killing your friend. And not clean either, not fast because they have the same problem, the same solution. So you tear each other apart, turn the rage at being chained up by these repellent psychopaths and the shitty lives waiting for you if you could escape against one another. You kill the pain by inflicting so much that you don't feel it anymore, the skin rips, the bones break, the scream rises and at the end of it you've both escaped the only way you can. One through death and one through blood-soaked transformation; your friend's last action to help you pummel the clay you're made from into a different, harder shape. Their reward is death and the defiling of their corpse in a manner that's as offhand as it is brutal. Your reward is getting ready to do it again. Forever. Until you die.

Horror, six different ways, rendered from a story that's, from a distance, just a fight. But it's never just a fight. That's what Lansdale shows us here and that's the one scar that will never, ever heal. Nor should we want it to.

"Fighting for peace is like screwing for virginity."
George Carlin

August

Apocalypse from the Outside

Pontypool, My Pontypool

*(This essay originally appeared on PseudoPod episode 345, "**Boxed**" by Donald McCarthy, narrated by Alex Rudy on August 2nd 2013)*

It's been a rough couple of months for my professional self-esteem. Anyone who's followed my blog may have noticed. Without going into detail, my professional worth, and the connection between what it is and what I think it is has been challenged, and extended, several times. It's not been pleasant, at all, and whilst some of it is the price of admission for being a freelancer, some of it has just been plain old bad luck.

Professional failure, emotional hurt, is a lot like a tree falling in a forest when no one's there, only involving far more Depeche Mode albums on repeat. If I erased the jobs I went for and was passed over for, if I erased the whistling sound as opportunities I thought were mine hurtled past on their way to other people, surely my head would be clearer. I could function better, think more, work past the assumption that very few of the people I write for actually value me (By the way if you're one of those people, and worried that I'm talking about you, the fact you're worried proves I'm not). I could be bigger, better, faster, more explosions.

Thing is though, I couldn't. That line from *Star Trek V* 'No, I, NEED my pain.' is actually true. We struggle and try and fail, and we learn when we fail. No one has a perfect record and it's the failures which help us map just how tall the mountains of our triumphs are. I'm not saying it's easy, it's really, REALLY not. I'm also not saying I'm a fan of the process because trust me there is plenty in my head I sometime wish I could turn the volume down on. But I am saying it's necessary.

Which SUCKS.

Don't erase your failures, don't live in them either and don't for a second believe I'm better at this than you. I'm not. I've just run through a couple of walls this year, and trust me, if I can save you the headache, or at least hand you some spiritual aspirin, then I'm doing something right.

The Mushroom Cloud's Shadow

*(This essay originally appeared on PseudoPod episode 346, "**Prisoner of Peace**" by David Tallerman, narrated by Caith Donovan on August 9th 2013)*

David's story speaks directly to two levels of horror; the hideous damage done by the Hiroshima and Nagasaki bombs and the consequences of that damage on the global psyche. We decided to run this story on the anniversary of the attack, because it was a possibility that had been raised by David on submission, He mentioned that whilst the story is set in Hiroshima, there are visual cues from both cities, specifically the one-legged Torii gate which, David told us, was from a photo of Nagasaki.

That photo I haven't seen. The one I haven't been able to stop looking at is the one of the mushroom cloud over the city. It looks wrong on a level that transcends the endless moral debates about the attacks, a manmade structure dwarfing the landscape around it, deceptively tranquil but defined by and marking a level of destruction the planet hadn't seen used in war prior to that. It's borne out by the comparison photos of ground zero before and after the attacks, the landscape rendered down to something clinical and scoured from the air, even though on the ground nothing was so simple, or orderly.

That cloud works as both metaphor and structure, for this particular moment in history. The detonation itself was brutally simple, and brutally effective. It looks precise, even clean, especially when viewed from a distance. Up close it breaks down, becomes granular and you can see the tens of thousands of people whose lives it ended or changed. The scientists, the air crews, the victims, the survivors, their families, the people of Japan, the soldiers whose lives were spared by the Japanese surrender. Countless lives all coming to a point, or an end, at ground zero. The shockwaves echoing down through history, the cancelled attacks, the bombs that didn't fall, the birth of the nuclear age, the Cold War, Mutually Assured Destruction, Glaznost and on down to the present day. Everything changed because of those two attacks and it's all too easy to debate their morality, to look at the cloud but not what it's made up of. David's story drags the focus away from the big picture, denies us the luxury of distance and makes us see them. The victims. The survivors. The people. We're still under the cloud's shadow and always will be. But now we can at least use our distance as context instead of as a shelter that will, at any moment, be ripped away.

"The bomb was not only dropped on the citizens of Hiroshima and Nagasaki. It was dropped on the whole of humanity."
Satoru Kanishi,

Trial and Discipline

*(This essay originally appeared on PseudoPod episode 347, Flash on the Borderlands XVI: Trial & Discipline. Featuring "**Passing Grade**" by Paul DesCombaz, narrated by Kyle Akers, "**The Killing Machine**" by Karen Runge, narrated by Eve Upton, and "**Awaiting Redemption**" by Maurice Broaddus, narrated by Laurice White on August 2nd 2013)*

Discipline, sometimes, is not moving. Discipline is sometimes staring the thing that will break you in the eyes and deciding that it won't break you forever, or, at the very least, you'll make it work for the meal. There's no such thing as a good clean fight but there's something like victory in leaving everything on the field.

We asked Karen to tell us about the story and here's what she said;

"When we are guilty of evil, do we deserve empathy? When we are victims of evil, are we capable of feeling empathy for those who have harmed us? Just how much punishment is too much? Where exactly do we draw the line between justice and cruelty?"

This one's going to stay with me for a while because it follows a brave, very unusual path. There's some very subtle narrative Aikido being done here, as Karen not only makes us complicit through the format of the story but also hides the true horror of what's going on behind two curtains. The first is the increasingly self-righteous, biblical language used in addressing the prisoners and the second is the rage everyone who's ever been the victim of a crime or been bullied or manipulated by someone else feels. We want to push back. We always want to push back but the moment we do we find ourselves faced with an incredibly complex piece of emotional algebra. How far is enough? How much is too much? Humanity is entirely too comfortable putting a boot on the throat of anyone who disagrees with us and, surely, if the wrong is great the vengeance should be too?

This is precision, needlepoint horror, stretching out each revelation in a way I rarely see and it's chilling. Everything is two steps away from where we are now and that's so close you can see the serial numbers on the killing machine, hear the piped classical music. There's no mercy here, just vengeance, forever and the death of innocence. Trials aren't needed and discipline? Discipline is forever.

That idea; that you must suffer to be redeemed is one of the areas where religion has caused genuine damage to the human psyche. I'm a resting Catholic, which means I still spell it with a capital C but am coming up on one, tragic, visit to mass in 18 months. I've talked about this at length elsewhere, but when it comes down to it one of the things that means I need to keep my faith at a distance right now is simple; the idea that you have to jump through hoops in order to be redeemed.

Joking aside I'm a huge fan of Wheaton's Law, it's one of the purest forms of ethical guideline I've ever seen and it transcends a lot of the more obscure, and ridiculous, teachings of extreme religion in all its forms. And yes, all its forms includes the Christian Right. Especially the Christian Right. No one should have control of your life, of when you eat, sleep, pray, whether you pray or what you do other than you. If you want to subscribe to external religious frameworks to help with that, awesome. If you want to subscribe to external intellectual frameworks designed specifically in response to the religious ones. Also awesome. Know what you can't do?

Be a dick about it.

Your choices are yours. Everyone else's choices belong to them and if you define yourself by inflicting discipline on others? You define yourself as the absence of freedom. There's no room for that sort of discipline, nor should there ever have been.

'...do you understand, sir, do you understand what it means when you have absolutely nowhere to turn?"
Crime and Punishment, Dostoyevsky

Alone in a Crowd of Loners

*(This essay originally appeared on PseudoPod episode 348, "**The Easily Forgotten**" by Philip M. Roberts, narrated by Laura Hobbs on August 23rd 2013)*

With a couple of notable exceptions, most of the conventions I've gone to have been different levels of okay. Don't get me wrong, if you drink, if you're a writer, then a lot of the conventions on the circuit are MASSIVE fun, that much is certain. But from the moment I first walked into FantasyCon and realized it was 300 strangers who knew one another getting drunk together, again, I realized something; I'm a man without a country.

I understand the allure of the outsider mindset, God knows I do. I classify myself as a journalist and a writer and those two groups define themselves as looking at society from the outside. That way we can point you all at the good movies and from time to time either berate you about how wrong you are, tell you what will give you cancer this week or couch barely-disguised character assassination in terms of being concerned for a famous person's weight.

Not that I do any of that. It repulses me in fact, but even journalists who actually show up to work are, by definition, outsiders.

Being an outsider gives you the ability to see not only how the sausage is being made but who's feeding what in where. It's like those tricks Penn and Teller used to do where they'd rebuild a piece of equipment out of transparent plastic and then perform it again so you can see everything.

But you can't actually engage. Everything around you is distanced, passive.

And you're alone.

Because when you're an outsider, you can see the pack but you're not of the pack and that's as liberating as it is dangerous. The thing here, whatever it is, is one of the subtlest fictional predators I've ever seen. It rides someone into the house, waits for the inevitable and then cheerfully cuts these people off from everyone but the increasingly psychotic leader who's killing them. I have no idea why it's doing this and it doesn't matter. What matters is seeing a fractional outsider society trying to pull itself together even as every one of its weaknesses and vagaries, everything that makes it human is exposed to everything that will do its absolute best to see it destroyed. There's no help, there's no one coming and there's no way to go because when you drift too far out from the pack, as these people have, the only thing you can do is survive or wait for something to decide you don't have to. A predator, a disease, an infection vector or just plain boredom. It doesn't matter and it never will because this sort of isolation is somewhere to live but not stay. The pack may be the pack, but there's safety in there, as well as the risk inherent in growing through interacting with others. Trust me, that's a risk worth taking.

'THIS HOUSE IS NOT SAFE'
The East

Widdershins: Protective Magic and Norman Partridge's "The Apotropaics"

*(This essay originally appeared on PseudoPod episode 349, "**Apotropaics**" by Norman Partridge, narrated by Matt Franklin on August 30th 2013)*

Apotropaic magic is protective magic. The word is derived from the Greek *apotrepein* which means to ward off, and that in turn is broken down to *apo*,meaning away and *trepein*, meaning to turn). It's also one of the most common forms of magic, and belief, even today. Evil Eye medallions are apotropaic magic items, good luck charms sold at shrines? Apotropaic. Dreamcatchers? Subtly different approach but still apotropaic. Charm bracelets, crossing fingers, knocking on wood, turning thricewise widdershins, not listening to a particular song at a particular time, avoiding cracks to ensure your mother's continued spinal health, all of it is apotropaic. We don't quite make offerings to the Averting Gods anymore, like the Greeks did, but we're not that far away from it.

Everyone has rituals, even if they don't quite see it. Some people always park in the same spot regardless of how far away it is from where they're actually going, others will always put the comic they want to read most on the bottom of the pile, others will always order the same thing every time they go to a particular restaurant. All of its ritual, all of it is another charm on the bracelet society hands you at the same time it takes the Fisher Price version away.

That's what fascinates me, the grey, misty land around the border between the child and the adult. None of us know when we cross it, a lot of us cross back and forth over it but we all know once it's crossed. Innocence is something you notice once it's gone, the map of your life suddenly rendered down to a blank page that reads HERE BE DRAGONS,

BILLS AND EMPLOYMENT.

I've talked before about the crucible moments that everyone goes through and this is almost the only one everyone has in common. You never forget the first conversation you shouldn't have heard. You never forget your first brush with mortality and you never, ever forget the first moment you realize that the responsibility falls on you. It's an interesting, horrible moment that this story captures perfectly, but does so with a fantastically unsettling ambiguity. You could just as easily read the discussion of vampires as apotropaic magic, couching a pair of horrible events in terms which are horrifying but much easier to deal with than watching one of your parents beat someone to death. The preventative and protective magic of youth, a thin line of salt surrounding your suddenly diminished, finite safe place. There's two kinds of heroism here too; the first is the decision to be the one who stakes the vampire. The second is the decision to defend innocence which, now, you can see the edges of. Possibly foolish, but definitely brave. And tragically, irrevocably mature.

'PseudoPod was 12 going on 13 the first time it
saw a dead human being.
Stand By Me

September

Polite Lies

The Family Business

*(This essay originally appeared on PseudoPod episode 350, "**The Bungalow House**" by Thomas Ligotti, narrated by W. Ralph Walters on September 6th 2013)*

This one's for Tim Wells. Stay frosty, brother.

The architecture of interdependency at the centre of this story haunts me. The first level that strikes is the lead's ghoulish fascination with these awful places discussed in the monologues. On the one hand, of course, it's because they're all familiar but on the other it speaks to a very basic human need. The same one summed up by the line that made me fall in love with the band Garbage:

I'm only happy when it rains.
I'm only happy when it's complicated.

I had the pink audio cassette version of that album. It RULED.

The sentiment is the same though. It's what powers a lot of sensationalist media, across current affairs, entertainment and sport. As I write this, a reality TV talent show has kicked off its latest season in the UK and my twitter feed is full of people crowing about how awful it is. Earlier today, it was split roughly equally between those decrying the WorldCon business meeting as the last bastion of the anally retentive male white oppressor and those members of the meeting who are not male, not especially anally retentive people involved in the meeting getting increasingly snippy at the brush they were being tarred with. Scattered across all this is the UK media's ongoing frantic cultural algebra as to whether the government's motion to attack Syria being defeated was a good thing. On top of all that is the reaction from the US to President Obama apparently deciding to ask Congress' opinion on the US' military intervention.

There's good in each of those stories, on both sides. There'll be talented singers on the talent show, there are people who are neither sexist or racist dinosaurs at WorldCon and the law of averages says there has to be at least one principled, articulate politician somewhere in the UK and US constitution.

Suspension of disbelief, folks. It's what's for dinner.

There's good.

There's always good.

But we never allow ourselves to see it. Instead we see the bad, the awful, the risible. We roll around in the effluvia of our society and revel in our misery because when it comes down to it, that's what we've always done. People slow down as they pass accidents, people film fights in the street.

Undercutting all that is the three-way conflict at the heart of the piece. The first is, of course, that of the protagonist and the artist. I love how this is seeded across the story and I'm looking forward to seeing if anyone says they saw it coming in the feedback. I certainly didn't. I do find the way Ligotti approaches the separation of, if not church and state, then heart and mind, brilliant. The dominant one is the only one that can speak, the dominant one has little or no memory of the dormant artist and yet the artist is powerful enough to manifest to the dominant personality. Looked at this way, it's a story about a man's creative shackles starting to break and him being faced with a choice; embrace his talent and the chaos and change, that goes with it or put his head back down and stay as who he is. Framed that way, this is almost the Joseph Campbell call to adventure, albeit with a little more of a body count than usual.

Except for the fact the lead and Dahla are so diametrically opposed. This is needlepoint precise horror, the way Ligotti takes our perceptions of Dahla and spins them through 180 degrees. She's not the traditional tragic horror woman, but rather a woman who finds herself in the middle of a very unusual situation and makes the best of it. We read about the horror. The horror comes into Dahla's gallery every afternoon and eats lunch. Imagine that constant, sustained, subtle, endless threat. No wonder she hates him.

Then there's the interesting collision between creativity and rationality we see here; twice. The protagonist works in a library; his job is literally to catalogue and order the creativity and combined knowledge of others. It's a hell of a job, I know a lot of librarians and they're all great people but it requires incredible discipline.

Compare that to the release of the artist both in the work he does and the implied murder of Dahla. Look at Dahla too, trapped between retail and art, creativity and realism. Three people, two bodies, two goals. No wonder the whole thing is unbearably tense. And that's even before we get to the questions that haunt me about this;

Where does the artist go when he records these journals?

What does he see?

How real is it?

The quote goes I will show you fear in a handful of dust. Ligotti shows us a universe of fear in nothing but a scratchy, faded audio tape and a hushed voice. As I said, it's an honour.

Not just to have Mr Ligotti here, but you as well. 350 episodes is a milestone. So much so that if this was a comic one of us would be dead, married, back from the dead or in a new costume by now.

That being said, we'd also all be two dimensional and four colour. So I think we're still ahead by the numbers.

Especially the number 350. For 301 (I'm contrary) weeks I've had the opportunity to come here, listen to the best horror fiction on the planet and talk to you about it. I joke about this being my dream job but it really, truly is. I love this. We all do. We wouldn't spend anywhere near as much time on it if we didn't. This podcast has grown into something rich and strange, a full fathom five's worth of darkness and light and humour and terrible, bone-liquefying horror. In the episodes I've been here I've learned more about horror, and myself, than I ever thought possible. Not the least of which is, I LOVE this weird, misshapen, occasionally boneheaded genre. I love SF and fantasy but…it's the difference between tea and good whiskey. I couldn't read nothing but horror but God DAMN if I don't get a shot of the best stuff on the planet once a week. I'll never stop being grateful for that.

BORN! IN THE I!O!M!

*(This essay originally appeared on PseudoPod episode 351, "**The Blues**" by Cameron Suey, narrated by Gabriel Diani on September 13th 2013)*

I went back to the Isle of Man for the first time in seven years a couple of weeks ago. It wasn't an intentional decision to stay away, I was just, in the words of Elijah Snow, busy. A lot of the time in the good way.

I was surprised by two things; firstly, how little emotion I felt when I stepped back onto Manx soil for the first time in almost a decade. You get a special kind of bond with your hometown, and when your hometown is a small scrap of land in the middle of the Irish sea, that bond becomes all the more pronounced. Because that way you don't get swept out to sea and, well, two of my best friends are Coast Guards. They're nice guys. Don't really deserve the hassle.

In fact, that was the other thing that surprised me. We spent time with my sister and her boyfriend, who happily drove us around for a day and a half. Then, on the second day, we went and hung out with some of my oldest friends. Orry, Pete (Whose name is Alan but he's so inherently Pete-esque that even his mum calls him Pete), Scott, Cads and Neil. At least two of them had no belief whatsoever they'd live past 30.

At least one of the ones who expressed that thought is now married, respectable and has an amazingly cute baby son.

The bastard also has the exact same hair line he had 20 bloody years ago but I digress.

I was a little worried, because I've been off the rock for a few years. Not everything's been bad but everything's been off the island and you lose step with a community like that very easily.

It was awkward for about 4 seconds.

I have a sister on the Isle of Man. But I have a lot of brothers too, and hopefully next time we'll be able to catch up with the others too.

That unique sense of comfort you get from your hometown

is something that never quite goes away. It can't be all bad, because you're on the street where you had your first kiss, or the community centre where your first RPG group met or any one of a dozen other completely personal, trivial, immensely powerful touchstones. I spent two days doing exactly what these men do, checking in with old haunts, spending time somewhere comfortable. Getting reacquainted with the past.

Nowadays I live inland, in a large city. So large, in fact, it has a public transport system that isn't buses that stop every two and a half bus lengths, like York. Seriously, Nottingham's ace. It has trams and everything.

Put me back on the Isle of Man and I'll adapt pretty quickly. Put me back on the Isle of Man post-apocalypse and I'll be relegated to Fetcher From Tall Shelves inside three days. I'm not even being self-deprecating, the sort of survival skills that most post-apocalypse characters magically have are ones we all like to think we have but very few of us do. That's one of those unusual, often overlooked kinks of horror that Cameron Suey, with this story, absolutely nailed. Here's Cameron to sum it up;

"Among many people of my generation, there is a certain romance to the apocalypse, linked to a fantasy of survivalist self-sufficiency. But the vast majority of us have none of the skills required to keep ourselves alive indefinitely without the support networks of civilization. "The Blues" was my attempt at confronting and ruminating on the limits of our adaptability, something not often addressed in apocalyptic literature."

The fascinating thing is there's heroism here anyway. Not the sort of ragged-jacketed heroism you see in post-apocalypse flicks but the calm, resigned heroism of sitting down with the end to talk. There's tremendous courage in looking death in the face. There's even more in not letting it win just yet. It's not a hopeful story by any means but it's a very gentle, very sweet kind of horror. This is the way the world ends, with the heroic bystanders. We may not live. But we'll damn sure go out on our own terms.

'swim out past the breakers and watch the world die.'

Santa Monica by Everclear. Certainly one of my favourite songs, possibly my favourite song by them.

The Kicker

*(This essay originally appeared on PseudoPod episode 352, "**Enough with the Crazy**" by Emile Dayne, narrated by Joe Scalora on September 20th 2013)*

My old home town has an asylum in it. It's not called an asylum, I seem to remember it's called Bootham House, but that's definitely what it is. It's a place where, if you are too profoundly mentally ill to function in society, you can be treated. It's a beautiful country house on about three acres of land in the middle of a magnificently gridlocked cathedral city. It has really, really high fences.

Two things you need to know about Bootham. Firstly, it's one of a pair. Bootham is on one of the main thoroughfares into the city whilst the Priory is located on the main road into York University campus. And yes, both those locations have generated their fair share of urban myths. The tremendously talented painter who can't be allowed to talk to anyone about his work is one. The biggie is that, the story goes, you can check yourself in at any time in Bootham but they decide when you're free to leave. Unless of course your illness doesn't mean you're a danger to yourself or others in which case you're given day release.

There's a contradiction there. But you know what? I've had a really awful week and I trust you guys to dig it up yourself.

That's how I met the Kicker. The Kicker has wandered York for as long as I lived there. He may wander the streets still. He's a well-dressed, earnest man often wearing a green tweed jacket and a checked shirt. He strides around the city with tremendous purpose, kicking each lamp post twice on the front, once on the side, once on the back.

That's all he does.

All day.

The last time I saw the Kicker he was walking past lamp posts. His step faltered just a little but he was making it. Hope he's doing okay.

The point is this; everyone finds different ways to control

and define their reality. For some its substance abuse, for the kicker it's the same four kicks to the lamp post bottoms of York.

We all need it at times, that single point of the screen that isn't spinning and as long as you look at it you won't get sick. Or at least sicker. Sometimes holding the line is a victory. Sometimes it's the only victory you're allowed. And sometimes, like Cypher says, ignorance is bliss.

'And PseudoPod knows they cannot hurt you unless you let them.' Bad months for me are usually soundtracked by Everclear. This is from One Hit Wonder and no THIS is my favourite song by them.

Let's Misbehave

*(This essay originally appeared on PseudoPod episode 353, Flash on the Borderlands XVII: Keeping Up Appearances. Featuring "**Down by the Sea**" by Joe R. Lansdale, narrated by Corson Bremer, "**The Demon Fields**" by Keith McCleary, narrated by Kevin Hayes, and "**Pawn**" by Jaki Idler, narrated by Julia Rios on September 27th 2013)*

It's always there. Under courtesy, under the social peace treaties that get us all through the day. The voice that screams about how do what thou wilt shall be the whole of the law and that there's a new sheriff in town. The place where every petty annoyance, every half-formed thought goes because to say them out loud would be rude, impolite, cause all manner of horrors.

Society's cornerstone is lies and it is buttressed by the desperate need to keep things civil. Least said, soonest mended, never mind eh, all those phrases of tattered armour that we wrap around ourselves when other people hurt us. Or, that tie us down when we want to hurt other people physically, emotionally, mentally. It's always there. It's always awake. Never let it out. No matter what it promises?

It's always there. Everything you think you can't say, everything you know you can't say. Everything you want to say anyway. It gets worse when you're with someone because they see the best in you. They want you to be that person and so do you and suddenly, you can FEEL the walls, hear the chains creak. The voice senses how close it is to release and it just starts screaming and screaming and after a while it's all you can hear and then

You let it out

And so do they

And your claws rend and tear at each other for a moment, voices raised, cruelty proudly displayed and then it's tears and apologies and long talks and if you're very unlucky the voice, back in your head saying 'That was fun. Let's do it again.'

And if you're really unlucky, you can hear the voice in the

back of their head saying the exact same thing.

Build your barn strong. Build your fences high. Remember the courage is in trying, not succeeding.

Sometimes though, you find yourself in a very different place. One where the voice on the inside of your head isn't just making sense, it's telling you things you need to know in order to survive. Sometimes attention must be paid, sometimes the dogs of war are let slip rather than chew through their leashes.

That's when appearances don't matter anymore. When things change for the better as you realize that the voice is you, it's always been you and that means it'll always bring you home. You're not safe. You're never safe with it, but it'll always close the deal. So you use that realization to put it away again. It's you, you're it. Neither complete without the other. Always the Pawn. Always the Queen.

All the fallen angels
Roostin' in this place
Count back the weeks on worried fingers
Virgin mother whatserface
Fallen Angel by Elbow

OCTOBER

THE SILENT AND THE DEAD

The Family Business

*(This essay originally appeared on PseudoPod episode 354, "**The Eulogy of Darien Meek**" by Niccolo Skill, narrated by Rich Girardi on October 4th 2013)*

It takes a special kind of author to make me think 'What happens next?' at the end of a story about death. Not in the usual sense either, there's no sense of this being a comfortable afterlife or even an uncomfortable one. This is a weaponized family and that concept by itself is bad enough.

It's also a neat twist on the two strands that lie at the centre of this story; mortality and family. Because this is a story about death, that's for certain. In particular it's a story about the curious pantomime of expectation and theatre that every funeral becomes. At first it feels odd, almost disrespectful and then you realize just what it is that's bothering you; funerals aren't for the person who died. Whatever you do or don't believe (And I'm not touching that one with a ten-foot pole) the person who's died has…died. They don't care what colour the casket is, how many tuna casseroles have been brought or how drunk anyone gets. They're somewhere else.

The funeral, the wake and everything that follows it. That's for the living. That's for us and that odd combination of emotional honesty and compassionate theatre is beautifully captured here.

The other thing that the story absolutely nails is the sense of family. A happy extended family is one that's extended geographically as well as numerically. It's nothing personal either but the more people there are in the family the more space they need. When something like this happens, that space evaporates and tensions can't help but rise. Again, that's really well captured here; the desperate need to be nice, balanced with the tension of the event and of being across from whoever you've been at war with in the family for God knows how long.

Then there's the horror. Three different kinds of it. The first is the simple, awful horror of death. Someone you love is gone. The only thing you can do is hurt. The second is the thing that sits inside the family and the fact that this happens every time there's a funeral. It should be absurd but instead it's tired and desperate and human. A funeral should be a chance to mourn your loved ones, not prepare to kill them a second time.

And that's the third kind of horror here; the denial of closure. No strange aeons have passed but death is denied to the Meeks and, worse, there's something waiting for them as soon as they pass on. There's no closure, no peace, just the horrific task of killing something wearing someone you love. And, perhaps, trying not to think about what could have happened to their soul.

Death is not the end. And sometimes that's not a good thing.

'I'm done with elephants and clowns.
Wanna run away and join the office.'
Mike Doughty, American Car, from the 2005 album Haughty Melodic

The Price

*(This essay originally appeared on PseudoPod episode 355, "**The Chair**" by Leah Thomas, narrated by Justin Riestra on October 11th 2013)*

"There's a price."

It's a line from a late run episode of *The West Wing*, where one particular character pushes themselves far too far for an admittedly very good cause. Just three words but those words have weight and heft to them like few others. He pays that price for most of the rest of the series and does so gladly. At least until the time comes for it to be collected.

As fictional characters, so real people. It's so easy to push too hard and too far for too long. So easy to pour your heart and soul into something and not realize that what you're doing is emptying everything that makes you who you are, into something or someone else. It's selfless but selflessness is one of those few positive traits that I think has got entirely too good a press over the years.

Because when you lose yourself you lose every boundary, every unique marker that makes you who you are. Also, let's face it, unswerving dedication to an ideal, or a company or anything, is fundamentally very dangerous. You lose all scepticism, all ability to make an informed decision.

They gain a follower. Or fuel.

You lose everything.

I'm not saying shut yourself off in an ivory tower either because that's no way to live, trust me I know people who have done that. I've rented space in one myself. What I'm saying is this; no job, no organization, nothing outside the people you love deserves your undying loyalty. Like the lady says, if that's what you see then you have to look with better eyes than that.

Your sense of self is the omnitool that unlocks the world and lets you put it together on your terms. It's also the dividing line between you and the rest of the world and it's a line each one of us crosses multiple times. We throw ourselves headlong into our work, our hobbies, our love lives, always looking for that moment where, 45 minutes later, the credits roll.

They never do. The curtain never falls. The music never stops. So make sure you have a good dance partner and know when, and that you are allowed, to leave the floor

'…I looked in that box just a second ago, and there was nothing there.
Sneakers, 1992

Stop the Press

*(This essay originally appeared on PseudoPod episode 356, "**The Night Wire**" by H. F. Arnold, narrated by Eric Luke on October 18th 2013)*

I've been privileged in the journalists I've known over the years. Stephen Hunt got me my first job as a 150 word a time film reviewer for no reason other than he'd heard me talk. Richard Whitaker, one of my best friends, worked his way up from a proto-blog (The Fulford and Tang Hall Lane Curmudgeon, which is STILL UP!) to being about half the staff at the *Austin Chronicle*. He's a regular at FantasticFest and once proudly told me Rick Perry's office would only talk to him if he started the conversation with 'Hello, it's Richard from the Chronicle, this is a legal matter.'

And then there's Donovan Farnham, who talks nineteen to the dozen and is the single most laconic human being I've ever had the privilege of meeting. Donovan's brand new, where Steven and Whit are both veterans but all three of them have the same quality to them; that distance, that willingness to observe not just something but how their reactions to it define or alter the story. Donovan was working the news wires during the horrific attack in Boston and I talked to him at a family wedding not long afterwards. His response was amazing; clear, unequivocal horror at the events mixing with wide-eyed amazement that he'd been on duty when it happened. He'd stood there and watched as the accounts had spooled off the wires, reacted with everyone else as his editor put him to work and did the thing all truly great observers do; reported without commenting.

It has a cost, this approach. That's something I saw in Whit's eyes when he told me about the prostitutes that had worked the red-light district near one of his first jobs. He said you could always tell when a girl wasn't liked by her colleagues because no one wrote down the number of the car she got into.

There's a line from *A Few Good Men* that I love completely. It applies to these three friends of mine and to so much horror fiction:

'They stand on a wall and say nothing's going to hurt you, not on my watch.'

Great journalism is nothing less than the ability to inform and through that, protect the people you're informing. Like GI Joe himself once said, knowing is half the battle and journalists, the ones who are worth a damn, have been fighting that battle for decades. There are always casualties, and often they're not immediately apparent. Even then though there's the story, just like before, just like after. The fog is always rolling in somewhere and the first people to tell us about it are always the journalists. Not just the hero either but the unnamed, heroic telegraph operator in Xeberica. Observing the end of the world, reporting it, because that way you can control and confine the awful, just long enough to warn other people it's coming.

Done wrong, journalism is worthless, evil. Done right, journalism is heroic. Here's to more of the right than the wrong.

'F. Scott Fitzgerald once wrote, "The rich are different than you and me." They sure are. They got more money.'
Kolchak, The Night Stalker

The 2013 Halloween Parade

*(This essay originally appeared on PseudoPod episode 357, "**Growth Spurt**" by Paul Lorello, narrated by Steve Anderson on October 25th 2013)*

This year's parade is in altogether colder climes. It's still pleasant weather but the sun sets hurriedly, as though late for an appointment, and the shadows that form have eyes, and teeth, and the most beautiful voices you've ever heard. You buy your hot chocolate, catch up with the churros guy, and find a good spot.

This year the past is first, an acknowledgement of either its importance or the fact there are some things that must be appeased rather than honoured. A welcome new addition this year, if you can call it that, are the cave paintings. Flowing with inhuman frame rates, they are tall, white, silent figures surrounded by chalk flames and distorted animals. Some of the animals look familiar, others do not.

(The Cave of Lost Dreams is the first time Werner Herzog worked out he could have just as much grim, teutonic fun with nonfiction as he could with fiction. It's an amazing film and, if you can, see it in 3D. Detailing research into the cave paintings found in Chauvet in France it's an extraordinary visual journey)

Behind them walks the woman. Tall, precise, elegantly tailored suit, black leather gloves. This year she has an honour guard. On one side of her, two men; middle aged, one balding and with glasses, one with a smirk and blood covering his face. Both are smartly dressed, both are arguing good-naturedly. Both have clearly been dead a long time.

(If you asked me what my favourite horror movie was I would say Cabin in the Woods. Like spiritual successor Get Out it's a film which you can analyse for days. Massively fun, incredibly dark and a regular feature on the parade)

The two teenagers on the opposite side of her stare into space, clutching each other, like animals separated from their mother far too young. You're sure the woman will be happy to fill that role for them.

(That strange wisdom didn't work out too well, huh Marty?)

Behind them come the police officers. The poor police officers, always on the front line, always the first to fall. The female sheriff is talking animatedly to the precise gentleman in the old-fashioned coat and older-fashioned French accent. On the rooftops nearby, a bestial figure lopes along keeping pace with him. Behind it, unobserved, something far too large to be a man prepares to strike.

(I figured Sheriff Jody Mills and Dupin from The Murders in the Rue Morgue would have a lot to talk about)

Next to them are the two men from the long-forgotten future. One is older, blond, wearing a leather trenchcoat and sneer that cops in '90s movies got issued with their badges. His partner is tall, precise, well dressed and clearly jacked to the nines. He's double fisting coffee whilst chewing on what seem to be large toffee pebbles. Clearly the price of freedom is eternal vigilance. Or at the very least, eternal caffeinating. Behind them, the polite Edwardian dead man smiles and looks at his feet.

(Split Second! Split Second is NOT a good movie. AT ALL. It features Rutger Hauer, Neil Duncan and Kim Cattrall battling a monster that may or may not be Jack the Ripper in a flooded post-climate change future. It is a tremendously fun time and one of the movies I used to cheerfully mine for Cyberpunk RPG sessions. I figured I could at least throw the two cops from it a solid here).

(The Edwardian dead man is the lead from glorious Vertigo horror comic, The Deadwardians.)

The scientists follow next and this is always a good float. The many Frankensteins and many monsters are front and centre and, somehow, have been able to not try and kill one another long enough to make a decent show of it. You even see one Frankenstein and his 'son' swap places regularly; monster and scientist changing places, working in tandem. It won't last, it never does but it's nice to see them trying.

(All the various Frankensteins, with a special guest appearance by the Danny Boyle-directed stage version. This featured Jonny Lee Miller and Benedict Cumberbatch as the Monster and Frankenstein, swapping regularly between the two depending on

what night you went. It, along with Richard Schiff's solo show Under the Lintel remain one of the only theatrical productions I'm genuinely sorry I missed.)

Behind them, the intense young man with the syringe and the basket is deep in conversation with the amiable Middle-Eastern scientist holding a rotting pumpkin. Next to them, wearing the battle armour of the University lecturer, a young man with precision cheekbones is deep in discussion with an older gentleman. The older man is holding forth at length about the true nature of the Earth and spiritualism and the younger gentleman is viewing him, and the entire conversation with something approaching bemusement.

(That is of course Duane Bradley from Basket Case, classic '80s shlock horror. He's talking to Doctor Bumba from tragically underappreciated and truly glorious sitcom Better off Ted. Accompanying them is Professor Challenger from Conan Doyle's Challenger stories and Edward Malone, the chronicler of his adventures.)

Next to them, two reporters frantically make notes. The older one, hat perched high on his head, writes by hand. The younger; taller, dressed more contemporaneously, simply holds out a digital recorder. There's a family resemblance and it's nice to see work like this shared between the generations.

(Kolchak the Nightstalker! Tireless pursuer of the supernatural and, I choose to believe, a man whose work inspired every monster hunter that followed him. His colleague is his younger self from the short-lived but fun reboot).

The reunion comes next. A hundred high school students, some dead, some alive, none of them caring. They dance and whirl each other around a little maniacally but with such tremendous joy at being here, at being *alive* enough, that it doesn't matter. Walking in their centre, the tall young man with an eyepatch waves and mugs. On one side of him, a shorter blonde woman is clearly overcome at the welcome she didn't expect to get. Next to her, her short, red-haired friend punches her in the arm and shakes her out of it. They wave in unison.

(Every kid who ever appeared in a high school slasher. And Xander, Buffy and Willow front and centre.)

Behind them, the twinned walls of trench coat-clad vampires walk in lockstep. The blonde one mutters something and, out of nowhere, the blonde mage appears beside him. The pair look at one another, the blonde vampire makes a joke about them sharing a tailor and bums a smoke. They laugh and start chatting as on the other side, the dark-haired vampire finds himself deep in conversation with the dark-haired woman who has appeared out of the crowd. They both carry themselves a little nervously, as though they don't trust themselves around people. They both bolster the other simply by being there. The vampire smiles, nervously at first but it widens to a full-blown grin as others join him out of the crowd. The warrior first, then the academic, both grizzled by events but both there, both able to make their peace. The woman with blue hair follows them both out of the crowd, still unsure of the situation but clearly knowing where she wants to be. Others follow them; the three boys, the absence that speaks of a ghost and the smell of old books, tea and Clash records. They are together, a glorious, shamblingly dysfunctional family of loners. None of them know where they go from here. None of them care. The recently dead boy and his girlfriend join them. They fit right in.

(Spike! John Constantine! Angel! Faith! Gunn! Wesley! Illyria! The three nerds! Giles was dead the year I wrote this! The two leads from Warm Bodies!)

AC/DC blasts out of the speakers and the next section of the parade arrives. The brothers and the car are a centrepiece every year but this year things are a little different. They have no one in the back seat but a legion of people keeping pace with the car. The battered man in the trenchcoat on one side, the immaculate king of Hell on the other. Behind them, legions of people walk unsteadily, as though not quite comfortable with their limbs yet. At the far edges of the parade, the brother and sister with the impossible weapons walk point. They know others will get the attention tonight. They know that works in their favour.

(The Winchester boys are IN THE HOUSE. Castiel and Crowley in the back seat. Behind them, a legion of the newly possessed. On the edges, Hansel and Gretel from the 2013 movie.)

Behind them, four other muscle cars move silently in formation, their windows down. The owners smile and wave at the crowd, aside from the last one. He simply looks, and waits, and dreams of deep dish pizza.

(The four muscle cars of the apocalypse. I LOVE Supernatural.)

The family float is a new addition and based on this year, it still has a few kinks to work out. The preppy teenagers wearing masks and other people's blood that surround it clearly aren't getting on with the people wearing animal masks, and the two groups barely tolerate each other's presence. The families on the float aren't doing much better. A mother, a father and two children clutch improvised weapons in one corner whilst across from them a woman with jet black hair and almost no patience tries to persuade her two little girls to come towards her. The ratcheted, spasming figure behind the two girls screams and the float is covered in moths for a moment. Uncaring, a nearby man with long hair tapes magazines around his forearms and looks nervously at the zombie float behind them. His gaze meets that of the woman with the katana and the jawless zombies in chains. He looks away first. Behind her though, the crossbow hunter with the poncho and the permanent sneer locks eyes with him. The crossbow hunter nods, slowly, once and the man relaxes a little. On the other side of the zombie float, the sheriff stares blankly into space. His son's eyes are dead and black behind him.

(Okay, in order. The two groups in masks are rival Purge groups. The family with improvised weapons are the family from the original The Purge. The woman with jet black hair and the two kids is from Mama. The man with long hair is Gerry Lane from World War Z who is making eye contact with Michonne from The Walking Dead. Behind her is Daryl from The Walking Dead. I lost my notes for this one but the Sherriff is, I'm sure, Rick. I'm not entirely certain why Carl is dead though.)

The last float in the parade this year is another family, but this one is, superficially, a little calmer. The small boy at the centre of the float is proud and happy, waving to the crowd and showing off the little creatures he's been growing. Their teeth are so white you can see them from where you're sitting. Behind him his father is waving but his grin is fixed. His mother simple stares out at the crowd. You get the sense there should be someone more. You get the sense that there is something awful beneath this family, that their position in the parade is one of both honour and fear. Keep the little boy at the back, keep as many people between him and his creatures and the rest of the world as possible. Keep them from growing.

(The family from the story which, three years on, remains one of my favourites)

Delay the inevitable. At least until next year.

'Goddamn creatures of the night. They never learn.'
The Crow, 1994

November

Layers

Operation Duvet

*(This essay originally appeared on PseudoPod episode 358, "**Apathetic Flesh**" by Darren O. Godfrey, narrated by Bill Roosum on November 1st 2013)*

There's a term in the UK; taking a duvet day. Basically, you call in sick even though you aren't, and you spend the day under your duvet. It surfaces every once in a while when the news has run out of other things to cover, and it's one of that legion of UK news stories which actually isn't one. It's just a statistic that arbitrarily gets words wrapped around it every now and again.

The temptation to make your life a duvet day can get pretty strong. We're all wrapped in cocoons of expectation and perception at the best of times; no one on my tram makes eye contact with anyone else for example. Likewise, at my day job, a lot of people use apologising to me for walking on the floor I just mopped as the social lubrication to get them from one end of the corridor to the other without ignoring me. Ask most of the people in the buildings I work in and odds are they couldn't describe me. I know I can only describe a couple of them.

The biggest blanket we wrap ourselves in though, is culture. And that's the one that I cling nice and tight to. I used to medicate with entertainment. I would go to the movies at least once a week, all year. Watch nine, ten shows religiously, own a wall of DVDs. Eight feet of shelving, doublestacked. It was armour, literally and metaphorically, turning the noise up so I didn't have to focus on the signal. It worked for a long time. Then when my life changed, it was no longer necessary.

I mention it here because I'm moving house. In fact, I'll be in the new place by the time you read this. We're moving to the other side of Nottingham and, as is always the case when we do this, there's been a purge of stuff. Moving country was a little like an air burial; I spent a week basically open housing friends to come in and take what they wanted. It was weirdly liberating, a little like attending your own wake and hearing people admire your stuff collection. Moving house is far less emotionally charged and far more logistically fun. Our shared DVD collections now fit in six binders and one of those is the computer games. It's a hell of a step down but I welcome it. There's a lot to be said for hiding in culture like that, but there's much more to be said against it. It's one step from hiding to cowering and the moment you cower, the moment you flinch, you become a victim. You don't have to be one, you just have to look like one for someone to notice and they will notice. If you're lucky, it'll be the jumpstart your system needs and the adrenalin will wake you up. If you're unlucky, then you'll find yourself cornered and forced to decide whether or not you really are a victim. Hell can be other people but the Hell that frightens me most is the one we make for ourselves. Even if it does have a duvet in it.

'...Mother is the name for God on the lips and hearts of our children.'
The Crow, 1994

Mephistopheles Checks Twitter

*(This essay originally appeared on PseudoPod episode 359, "**Face Change**" by Jeff Hewitt, narrated by Anson Mount on November 8th 2013)*

The old ways aren't the best, but they are the most enduring. Oh sure, there's a place for the theatre of it, some people get off on that. The witches at midnight. The cracks of thunder and lightning. The verse. The crossroads. The contract.

The blood.

But who carries a pen these days, let alone can be bothered to read the fine print? Humanity has stuff to do, places to go, Foursquare locations to conquer. So, the technology of damnation has to evolve and so Hell has embraced the attention economy.

Think about it, it makes perfect sense. We are at the bottom of a well of signal decades deep, constantly pushing out into space and never, once, escapable from the surface of the planet. It's why it always makes me smile when 'you can't stop the signal' is used as a rallying cry, firstly because it's true and secondly because that may not be a good thing.

Years ago, it was statistically figured out that *Star Trek* in some form is being shown somewhere on the planet all the time. These days it wouldn't surprise me if it was *CSI* and *NCIS*. William Peterson, Lawrence Fishburne, David Caruso and Mark Harmon bifurcated a million times over, a compound eye of dutiful men doing dutiful things whilst their staff slave away in endless techno-backed research montages.

Don't get me wrong, I love that stuff. But my point is that's fortunate, because it's everywhere. It's our air, our environment, our deep, dark woods. That makes it perfect camouflage for the things wearing men's faces that used to wander out of those woods and lead children away to a hillside that shouldn't open but does, just once, for them. They're the predators of fiction and myth, the tigers, burning bright, wearing sharp suits and being made fun of in Michael Bay movies. Our hunters, our icons. Don't make eye contact. Maybe they won't choose you this time. Also, I'd watch fewer infomercials if I were you. Y'know. Just in case.

The Roy Batty Moment

*(This essay originally appeared on PseudoPod episode 360, "**Anasazi Skin**" by Matt Wallace, narrated by Lance Roger on November 15th 2013)*

The reason so many people focus on Roy Batty's final monologue in *Blade Runner* is it's one of those moments of perfect, immutable cinema. Everything, Hauer's physical and vocal delivery, Ford's almost micro-expression acting, the set, the music, even the bloody dove, it's all perfect. I can think of maybe five moments like that across every single movie I've seen. It's what cinema is designed to do and, by definition, the sort of thing it can't do very often.

It's also loved because we're conditioned to run headlong from emotional honesty as far and fast as we can. Seeing Batty, who has done hideous things, be so open, so peaceful in his final moments is as idealistic as it is intimidating. He's a constructed person certainly but a person nonetheless, someone who has fought hard and long to stay alive, done questionable things (As he himself says) and in the end, loses. He has two choices; to rail against the world, go out kicking and screaming or to let it happen. To revel in both his time and the fact that time is finite. It's an extraordinary act of bravery to choose the latter, and that's something everyone, the actors, the characters, the crew, the audience, all get.

We run from that sort of emotional honesty because it's when we're weakest and we can't be weak. Weakness gets us noticed. Weakness gets us killed. Weakness shows people we've been hurt and proves we can be hurt again. Weakness makes us victims. And that goes double for guys in the west and triple for guys in the UK. Emotion gets you hurt. Emotion gets you mocked. The stiff upper lip isn't there because it's proper it's there because it's atrophied from being locked in place.

That's what we're taught.

We're taught wrong.

There are two levels of emotional honesty that Matt deals with here and both are near superhuman feats of bravery and strength. Simply being aware of how you feel is sometimes the hardest thing in the world. I used to have a friend who talked about his 'ignorance shield', that he could survive any long-term stress as long as he wasn't actually aware he was under stress. He's right too, the simple act of not making eye contact with the thing causing you stress is often enough to let you get by, at least for a while. Never, ever for long though. Sooner or later you have to turn and look it in the eyes and stare it down. You'll fail, the first couple of times, everyone does.

But you'll keep going.

Everyone does.

The second level of emotional honesty is much harder and much more rewarding; let people in. Lovers, friends, family. Trust people to get between you and the door every once in a while. Stop looking for the exit, stop looking for the punch that's being hidden, the barbed words being prepped.

They don't always come, because sometimes you find someone who feels and thinks the same way as you. Because sometimes when it's going badly, and trust me it does go badly, you'll lose a step and feel their back against yours. No one who will stand with you is undeserving of your time and your love. No time you spend standing with the people who matter to you is wasted no matter how small, no matter how brief. You will all fall. Some of you won't get back up.

But most of you will. And you'll remember those who haven't.

Be brave. Open up. Stand up. You're not alone.

" Come on and take your best shot, let us see what you've got.
Bring on your wrecking ball."
Wrecking Ball, Bruce Springsteen, from Wrecking Ball (2011)

The Great Dinosaur Rush

*(This essay originally appeared on PseudoPod episode 361, "**The Murmerous Paleoscope**" by Dixon Chance, narrated by Christiana Ellis on November 22nd 2013)*

The Great Dinosaur Rush took place between 1877 and 1892, and was both a huge expansion for the field and a near abject disaster. Marsh and Cope each resorted to bribery, theft and the destruction of finds to get one over on the other. Which when you think about it shows just how bad things had got. These men of science, dedicated to learning, wilfully destroyed possibly unique knowledge to ensure their rival didn't find it first. The fight got nasty, with actual fossil rustlers, artificially inflated prices and serious underhand dealings on both sides. This led to the eventual economic and social ruin of both men, even as their discoveries were lauded.

(And in 2017, to the release of DRAGON TEETH, a 'lost' Michael Crichton novel about the conflict)

There's definite parallels with the so-called Bone Wars here, and I love how Dixon folds those parallels in and out of the story. You get the idea of the higher intellectual authority moving what it perceives to be the lesser species around and there's a lot of chilling stuff there. I especially like how the steampunk element is used, pragmatically and without any show. This is just how these people work, and that makes the final scene, and the fight with what used to be Eccleston, even more horrible even though we see none of it. Everyone in the story is a chess piece, and none of them are as high-ranking as they think they are.

What really hits home is that power games like this have consequences, even for the people running them. In the real world, Cope and Marsh destroyed each other's reputations even as they helped cement palaeontology as a scientific discipline with popular interest behind it. Here, the two creatures, hopefully, prove to be the architects of their own destruction. The parallels between their attitude to the heroine and the attitude towards women at this time are also very neatly handled. Control breeds arrogance and complacency and those in turn breed exactly the kind of people tough enough to cease control for themselves, even at the expense of their own lives. Here's to the bone hunters, especially the women like Mary Anning, who gives her name to the lens used here and who, unlike the ultimately destructive Marsh and Cope, is unfairly overlooked by history. Digging the past out one bone at a time, and making the future as they did so.

"The worse the country, the more tortured it is by water and wind, the more broken and carved, the more it attracts fossil hunters, who depend on the planet to open itself to us. We can only scratch away at what natural forces have brought to the surface."
Jack Horner,
How to Build a Dinosaur: Extinction Doesn't Have to Be Forever

ONLY IF YOU RUN

*(This essay originally appeared on PseudoPod episode 362, "**Go, Go, Go Said the Bird**" by Sonya Dorman, narrated by Heather Welliver on November 29th 2013)*

There's a test sequence that's been released from the new Studio Ghibli movie. It's directed by Isao Takahata and is based on the *Tale of the Woodcutter*. The sequence shows a character running headlong across the world, breaking through walls, running up and down hills, their robes streaming along behind them. As they run, never slowing, they begin to lessen, their clothes and accoutrements leaving a comet trail behind them.

I'm fascinated because the sequence is completely ambiguous. It could be that the character is running towards some kind of freedom, the restrictions and obligations of their life falling away as they do so. It's as likely that they're running in a way which means they're lessened with each step. Every pace taking them not closer to home but further from themselves.

That's the first thing this story put me in mind of. There's the same headlong sprint through life here, the same rendering everything down to one single action; flight not fight. However, there's something else here; the brutal pragmatism of someone who's learned to survive as much as they've learned to live. The headlong run home is a huge signifier of something awful happening but, as the story goes on, Gorman shows us just how little shelter there is anywhere in the piece. Home is the place you hate the least. The place that may do you damage but it's familiar; a friendly wound, an understanding injury.

That's the real horror for me; the fact that somewhere like this is worth returning to. It's odd, for a story that's so bare bones minimalist, there's a lot of architecture. The gender expectations and the violence combined with the simple truth that any port in a storm is better than none. This isn't a run from escape, it's a run through a maze, and one that can only ever end one way. Why it ends that way is the one place where the story is truly open. I can see it being read as a condemnation of the parasitic nature of parenthood, of the place of women in society and as a reflection on mortality. I'm sure there are others, the elemental nature of the story certainly lends itself to them. As does its fluidity. Meaning is what you run towards. Whether you get there or not isn't something you always get to decide.

December

Approach, Focus

Something Approaches: The Friedkin Way

*(This essay originally appeared on PseudoPod episode 363, "**Footsteps Invisible**" by Robert A. Arthur, Jr., narrated by Kevin M. Hayes on December 6th 2013)*

William Friedkin, one of the greatest horror directors in history, described true horror as seeing something approach. The idea is that you cut away just as the awful is about to happen and the monster leaps from the screen, or the page, into the mind's eye of your audience. There it runs rampant, doing far more damage than you could ever hope to achieve on your own. The pictures are better on the radio, but the pictures are always bloodier in your mind.

Horror as absence haunts me. This story is a great example of how it works; we never see just who, or what, is pursuing Sir Arthur here and that triggers the same overactive imagination that the first approach relies on. It's tied to the implied vulnerability of someone missing a sense too, and that in turn springboards off into the third approach Arthur takes. There's a deleted scene in Guillermo Del Toro's *Mimic* that this put me in mind of. The new form of life the movie revolves around confronts the female lead and, for the first time in the film, speaks with a human voice. It says one word.

'Leave.'

True horror is seeing something approach. But true horror is also understanding - and facing - something that's already here. That in turn ties into the social unease of life in the city, especially for country mice. I'm 6'2 and built like a linebacker and very nearly every time I've been concerned for my safety has been in cities. There are, after all, a million stories there. And you're always the victim in some of them.

That unease, for me, is also tied to the idea of predation and Episode 363 plays with that idea on multiple levels. The physical hunt is explicit and the supernatural one is so wonderfully, chillingly implied by the final lines. The cultural predation here is, arguably, the most interesting element though. The past is fed on by the present here and the monster, the mummy, whatever you view it as, is a reactive force, nothing more. This is a story about an antibody, one that reacts to an intrusion but can't prevent it. In that regard, the creature is preyed on just as it preys on the hapless Sir Arthur. The only difference is the creature has nothing but time, whilst Sir Arthur has anything but. And both of them are just part of a larger ecosystem that eats and kills and repeats over and over, regardless of what they do.

True horror is seeing something approach. But perhaps it's also that thing not even noticing you as it passes by.

"Hey Benny! Looks like you're on the wrong side of the river!"
The Mummy, 2001

Something Approaches: Carved Across Reality

*(This essay originally appeared on PseudoPod episode 364, "**The Yellow Sign**" by Robert W. Chambers, narrated by B. J. Harrison on December 13th 2013)*

So Friedkin defines horror as seeing something approach. Or, from time to time, hearing it. That's a good definition too, especially with the implied cut away just before the horror truly begins.

But here, the whole point is you don't see it approach. Here horror is, not even blindness, but a subtle rewiring of your brain, something that sits in your blind spot. This is horror as cuckoo, sitting in the middle of your nest and demanding to be fed as though it belonged there. It's a really subtle take on the genre, and one that I could stand to see in lots of other places. In fact, if this reminds me of anything, it's *Pontypool.* An excellent movie about the infection of a small Canadian town by a linguistic virus, it's a story that has a lot in common with this one. There's the same creeping sense of something being wrong, the same feeling of the world being rebuilt around you and the same nagging sensation that your blind spot can see you just fine and it's only getting bigger.

Like the last story, this piece is about being hunted. However, here the hunter is an idea and no one can outrun those. Wrapped in an exploration of what happens when the relationship between artist and model, and artist and work, collapses this is a story that wears its years lightly and still packs a hefty punch. Forbidden knowledge, broken people, a story that shouldn't be told but somehow always is and underneath all that, the Yellow King, his roots gnarled and skeletal, reaching up through decades of horror, taking in literature, film, TV and finally, podcasting.

The King in Yellow is here. He's always been here. And we'll always be in the audience.

Something Approaches: Whispers in the Dark

*(This essay originally appeared on PseudoPod episode 365, "**Whispers in the Dark**" by Andrew Marinus, narrated by Graeme Dunlop on December 20th 2013)*

The removal of a sense is a peculiar kind of horror all by itself. I've talked before about how there's always an instinct to jump, to push, to unfetter yourself from rationality and do the thing the back of your brain is screaming at you about. The healthy version of that instinct leads to adrenalin sports. The unhealthy side leads to everything from bar fights to addiction and death.

What Andrew does here that I think is especially clever is combine that instinct with a beautiful workaround for the traditional horror monster problem. Because monster horror writers have to constantly walk a fine line between showing you too much and showing you enough to know how much trouble the character's in. It's a very difficult line to walk, especially as there's often a very large, angry thing on one side of it, but Andrew does two things here that sidestep every problem. The first is that this apocalypse has already happened and has been happening for a while. It's a smart move, allowing him to give the story real immediacy. That's backed up by the way we never see the plants, just see - and hear - what effect they have. Perhaps true horror isn't seeing something approach, but knowing it's standing just outside arm's reach, waiting for you to open your eyes....

That image of the patient, whip smart hunters, would be terrifying enough on its own. But the cherry on the sundae of doom here is the way in which every possibility has already been run through. You can't tunnel under them, you can't look at them and you can't go near them because they'll find you and do something impossibly horrific to you as you die. There's no square-jawed hero, no last minute two-fisted scientific breakthrough. There's just the end, whether you wait for it to come to you or you run at it, eyes wide, your personality falling away like the wings of Icarus as you die. No bravery, no sacrifice, just them, waiting. Forever.

Happy Christmas !

"First of all, keep him out of the light, he hates bright light, especially sunlight, it'll kill him. Second, don't give him any water, not even to drink. But the most important rule, the rule you can never forget, no matter how much he cries, no matter how much he begs, never feed him after midnight."

Gremlins

Something Approaches: To Build A Fire

*(This essay originally appeared on PseudoPod episode 366, "**To Build a Fire**" by Jack London, narrated by Wilson Fowlie on December 27th 2013)*

Your focus shrinks in a crisis. The unconscious processes you trusted your body to deal with all become overt. You breathe like you would normally, you walk like you would normally but every single motion is conscious. You're aware of everything, as the fight-or-flight instinct at the back of your mind screams at you to do one or the other, and do it *now*. It's even worse if it's long-term stress because after a while you find yourself so aware of everything you do, you're no longer yourself. You're an actor playing a role, badly, and it's only a matter of time before your audience notices, or you forget your lines, or you fly apart at the seams.

Stress. Trauma. Crisis. None of these kill straight away. All of them grind you down, blunt the edge of your mind. All of them do almost irreparable damage and all of them can be survived. Sometimes survival is all it is, but you can survive, you can endure almost anything. There's a human instinct that encourages us to give in, to test ourselves to destruction. We want to see what happens when we get too hurt to continue, when we run off the edge of the world, and sometimes we do just that.

But that isn't the horror that sits, patiently, just outside the dwindling fire in this story. This isn't horror that's approached, this isn't even horror that's been seen. This is horror that's kept pace with you the whole time, knowing when you'll fall long before you do. This is horror, once again, as predator rather than monster. There's hope here, but it's hope with an expiration date. You can't win. But you can go down swinging as your focus drops from the mechanical processes of life to the mechanical processes you can afford to throw away, to, finally, waiting for the end.

Make it work for its meal. Make it sweat. Make it bleed if

you can. It's worth it.

Especially as sometimes you can kill it before it kills you. Sometimes you get rescued too. Make no mistake, that's what you did for us this year. Three months ago, I was mentally drafting the last ever outro for PseudoPod. The fact I didn't have to write it is entirely down to you. The fire had gone out, we were dying, and you came and got us. From each of us, to each of you, thank you.

That was 2013 for me. A year where I worked harder than I ever have before. I'm exhausted. We all are. But we're ready for what's next, the fire's burning and we've got backup. So, from all of us, and me, thank you for 2013 and thank you for 2014 too. We'll see you there next week but until then PseudoPod wants you to remember one thing.

This year, you were fantastic. And you know what? So were we.

See you in the future. Happy New Year everyone.

No direct quote but this is a riff on the Ninth incarnation of Doctor Who's regeneration scene. Who knew a gobby Northern Time Lord would hit me right in the brain huh? Oh yes. EVERYONE.

Hello everyone! Welcome to the Appendix!

So, it turns out this was a year where I experimented with fewer end quotes and with not writing the sources for the ones I did use. Fun! So, here are the missing end quotes, arranged by month. If you recognize any, do let me know at @AlasdairStuart.

January

"ONLY way you can possibly lose is if you wake the next morning and you're the same person as you were before."

March

"We see what nobody else does."

"The hero is not always the strongest man, sometimes it's the just the guy who leads the way."

"You can't be a hero without being a coward."

April

"As the crow flies, the wolf will hunt."

June

"Know that was a penny for your thoughts. If they are as confused as mine, perhaps sharing them will help."

October

"Anything you see of us before then is a hallucination…"

November

"Welcome to the New Atlantis. This is where you die."
(I have a hole in my notes here so any ideas, get in touch. It's a nice line though.)

'....they rode like fire across the prairie and it could never have been fast enough.'

(Again, nothing in my notes here but what a beautiful turn of phrase!)

CPSIA information can be obtained
at www.ICGtesting.com
Printed in the USA
FFHW010318100219
50486891-55730FF